GARDENING IN IOWA AND SURROUNDING AREAS

A Bur Oak
Original

GARDENING IN IOWA
AND SURROUNDING AREAS

VERONICA
LORSON
FOWLER

WITH THE

FEDERATED GARDEN CLUBS

OF IOWA

UNIVERSITY OF IOWA PRESS
IOWA CITY

University of Iowa Press,
Iowa City 52242
Copyright © 1997
by the University of Iowa Press
All rights reserved
Printed in the United States of America

Design by Ken Carlson and Karen Copp

http://www.uiowa.edu/~uipress

Printed on acid-free paper

Library of Congress Cataloging-in-Publication Data
Fowler, Veronica Lorson.
    Gardening in Iowa and surrounding areas / by Veronica
Lorson Fowler with the Federated Garden Clubs of Iowa.
      p.   cm.—(A Bur oak original)
    Includes index.
    ISBN 0-87745-584-8 (pbk.)
    1. Gardening—Iowa.   I. Federated Garden Clubs of
Iowa.   II. Title.   III. Series.
SB453.2.I8F69   1997
635'.09777—dc21   96-49069
                                                    CIP

02   P   5   4   3   2

To the inspired creators of
the Reiman Gardens

Contents

FOREWORD

Members of the Federated Garden Clubs of Iowa are dedicated to aiding and encouraging civic beauty and the study of all aspects of the art of gardening. We can think of no better way to further that mission than to create a book about gardening in Iowa and donate the proceeds to Iowa State University's Reiman Gardens.

The Federated Garden Clubs also wants to help gardeners learn. Through the help of the Iowa State University Extension Service and other knowledgeable gardeners, our 2,300 members have gained experience in how to garden successfully in Iowa. We want to share this knowledge with others.

We hope the information in this book will be useful to all gardeners in Iowa and will be of special interest to beginning gardeners and those new to gardening in Iowa. It is with pride that we present this book for gardening in Iowa, the Beautiful Land.

BARBARA PHILLIPS RUSK
FEDERATED GARDEN CLUBS
OF IOWA, INC.

PREFACE

Gardening in Iowa is like gardening nowhere else.

Iowa is perhaps the only state where people brag not only about things like good schools and friendly folk; they brag about their beautiful black dirt, too. (Oops. I mean soil, of course. As Iowa soil aficionados have often reminded more than one gardener new to the state, don't demean the lovely, rich stuff by calling it dirt.)

Gardeners living west of Iowa are envious of our plentiful rainfall. Southerners envy our cool summers which allow us to enjoy our gardens on all but the hottest July and August days. New Englanders, who have to pull more than a few boulders out of most gardens, admire our stone-free soil. And gardeners to the north wish for a few more of our warm days.

That isn't to say gardening in Iowa is carefree. We have brutal, harsh winters that greatly limit what we can plant and that shorten our growing season. Since we're locked in the middle of a continent, we're vulnerable to breathtakingly rapid weather changes. Those late-winter thaws might give humans hope that spring is on its way, but they're devastating to perennials and many other plants. And lately, it

seems, we've entered into a weather cycle of extremes. Each year, new batches of weather records are set. One summer might bring a baking drought and the next a flood.

What Iowa gardeners need is a book about gardening in Iowa—and this is that book. Other garden books give advice for the whole country or even the whole world. Those beautiful photos that you see in coffee-table books often are shot in Great Britain, a place with a climate so gentle and temperate that gardeners hardly know the words summer and winter. Throughout the following pages, you'll find tips by experienced Iowa gardeners, Federated Garden Clubs members who garden in all of Iowa's ninety-nine counties.

Gardeners live by the seasons, so this book is written in a month-by-month format, explaining concisely what garden chores should be done each month. Is this the time to apply that pre-emergent stuff for crabgrass? When should lilacs be pruned? Is it too early to plant peas? This book should answer all these questions and much more.

Not only will this book make you a better gar-

dener, your purchase of it will help others enjoy the special beauty and fascination of gardening. Royalties from sales of the book are being donated to the Reiman Gardens. The fourteen-acre Iowa State University gardens are located just south of the university's football stadium and include rose gardens, herb gardens, a wetlands area, and many other plantings.

There are many people who donated their time to this book. Ken Carlson, a talented Des Moines graphic designer, and Karen Copp of the University of Iowa Press came up with a beautiful, visually appealing design for the book and cover. Ames artist Patty McGrane Harms devoted hours of time and talent to create original illustrations for the monthly chapter openings, and Iowa City artist Claudia McGehee employed her gardening enthusiasm to draw the scratchboard illustrations used as spots within each chapter.

Thanks also to Jennifer Phelps, a *Des Moines Register* features copy editor and good friend, who gave up a lot of spring days to sit down indoors and edit copy. The book couldn't have been completed, either, without Janie Lohnes and Irene Pope, members of the Ames Garden Club, who spent hours sorting through the piles of horticultural tips mailed to us by Federated Garden Clubs members. Garden club member Linda Hodges compiled the list of Iowa gardens to visit and helped index the book, as did Denise Vrchota.

Iowa State University Horticulture Extension also contributed greatly to this book. Horticulture extension specialists were exceedingly generous with their time and materials in reviewing sections of the book, offering recommendations on the best plants for Iowa, and, as usual, dispensing sound gardening advice.

And last, but of course not at all least, my husband, Giles, who with his meticulous eye looked over page proofs and distracted our two children, Kate and Andrew, while their mother wrote this book.

JANUARY

JANUARY CHECKLIST

🌿 Make an overall garden plan for the upcoming year. List priorities to check off as you accomplish them.

🌿 Place orders for any catalogs. (See list of mail-order supply companies on page 136.)

🌿 Learn more about gardening by joining a garden club or signing up for a Master Gardener course. (See page 144 for more information.)

🌿 Place as many orders as possible for seeds and plants. Ordering early ensures getting the varieties you want.

🌿 Use calcium chloride, rather than sodium chloride, to melt driveway ice and snow. It's less harmful to plants.

🌿 Cut up your Christmas tree with hand shears and a saw and use the cuttings as a mulch around plants and shrubs.

🌿 Don't use softened water on your houseplants. It can result in browning of the leaves. Instead, melt snow, collect rainwater, or find another water source. Use tepid, not cold, water when watering.

🌿 Because houseplant growth is now very slow, don't fertilize your houseplants this month.

🌿 Remove dust from houseplants with a damp cloth or in the shower. Commercial plant polishes, milk, or other liquids can clog pores. Rinsing plants a few times a year also discourages spider mites and other pests.

- Keep houseplants away from cold window panes.

- Remove heavy snow from evergreens with a broom to prevent branches from snapping.

- Check any stored plant roots or corms, such as dahlias or glads, for excessive shriveling and decay. Remove any that are damaged.

- Start seeds of slower-growing herbs, such as parsley, thyme, tarragon, and sage. Don't be tempted to start seeds too early. Without lots of natural light and adequate heat (as in the climate of a greenhouse), they'll get leggy and diseased.

- Brussels sprouts planted last year can still be harvested.

- Take cuttings from ivies and other plants you're overwintering indoors. Root in jars of water on your windowsill. These can be planted outdoors later.

- Buy coleus, wax begonias, and other flowering plants for indoor decoration. Keep well watered and in bright light. Later, you can plant them outdoors as bedding plants.

- Bring in pots of bulbs for forcing. (See pages 100–101 for instructions on forcing.)

GARDEN DESIGN

T. S. Eliot was wrong. January, not April, is the cruelest month, at least for Iowa gardeners. Surrounded by glossy catalogs, magazines, and gardening books, we dream frustrated dreams of beautiful, flawless gardens, full of flowers and bountiful with vegetables. Our daydreams are interrupted, however, by the howling wind and the yellow flash of the snowplow scraping by.

But gardeners can tap the frustration of January and put it to good use. It's the month to bring out graph paper, measuring tape, a calculator, and all those catalogs to make grand garden plans.

An overall vision for your garden is essential. Without a long-term plan, you will have a rose bush here, a vegetable plot there, a couple of hostas in the back—all planted without any cohesive plan. You'll get a much bigger bang from your gardening budget and effort if you sit down for a few hours and decide exactly what it is you want to achieve in the garden.

You can design your garden yourself, or you can bring in a professional. Some greenhouses and nurseries provide landscape-design services. Many greenhouses and plant suppliers will come out to your house for no charge and make suggestions about what to plant where. These are fine for overall suggestions, but they are seldom as comprehensive as those for which you pay a flat fee.

There are a number of excellent firms cropping up in the state that specialize in landscape design and installment. The skills of these firms are as varied as those of an interior designer or hairstylist. When deciding whether to hire a firm, ask for a list of jobs it has done and visit the sites to see if the firm is what you're looking for.

Ask any landscape firm about implementing an overall landscape in stages and doing much of the work yourself. In their first year of developing a landscape, many people simply start with a design, then plant some key trees and shrubs. The next year they implement another chunk of the plan. They do more the third year, spreading out larger projects over five years or so.

To design a garden yourself, first look at garden books. Lots of garden books. Go to the local library and glut on gardening and landscaping books. Visit public gardens and home and garden shows. When possible, go on garden tours or get permission to snoop in the backyard of skilled gardeners in your area.

Do you want a formal garden, full of linear, geometric patterns and neatly trimmed hedges? Or do you want a loose, informal garden with blowsy wildflowers? Will you focus primarily on vegetables, or do you want a spectacular show of flowers—or both? Do you have lots of shade and yearn for a peaceful green shade garden, or do you want to prune the trees and shrubs and have a garden full of light?

Is your garden a place for children and pets to play? Or will it be a horticultural showplace that won't take such wear particularly well? Do you want to spend a lot of time puttering in the garden, or are you striving for low maintenance?

When you find photos of what you want, take notes on the plants. If possible, take the book to a copier that will make a color copy. After you have a general idea of what you want to do, get out in the yard and walk around. Look at your house and land as though there were nothing there and you could start from scratch. What would you do? Maybe it's time to cut down the overgrown yew bushes that block the view of the front living-room windows and plant something more manageable.

Take photographs of your garden and yard to help you see it more objectively. Ask friends or relatives whose taste you admire to give you a frank opinion of what needs to be done.

Make a bird's-eye sketch of your property. If you like, get precise and measure the boundaries. Draw in buildings and existing trees, shrubs, beds, and fences in black pen. Lightly shade in shady areas with a pencil and include the shade thrown by buildings. Draw what you want to add or note what you must change in red.

Then draw your home as viewed from the front, where visitors approach, and from the angle you approach it when you come home. Also consider drawing your garden from key viewing points, such as a kitchen window or deck. Draw existing shrubs, trees, and plants in black. Then draw in red what you feel should be added.

Include a utility area—a place for garbage cans, a dog run, and the like. If you have children, include an open area for play. Driveways and sidewalks are part of the landscape, and flowers and shrubs can be planted around these. Consider paths that will lead you and visitors from one area to another. Create a space to view your garden. This can be as simple as a bench or as elaborate as a deck or back porch. In Iowa, where mosquitoes are a nuisance, it's wise to screen in sitting areas.

Now, draw up a list of priorities. Don't expect to complete everything in one year. Most landscape plans take several years to complete. Really good gardens, like those you visit on garden tours or see in magazines, often take a decade or more.

Maybe a top priority is planting a privacy hedge. Maybe you need to install a flagstone path in a side yard where no grass grows and plant the rest of the area in a shade-loving ground cover.

Set a budget. It's easy to go to a greenhouse for some perennials and instead impulsively blow your flower budget on a lot of annuals that will be gone in a year. Instead of buying what's pretty in a greenhouse or catalog, buy only what fits into your overall plan.

Research the particular plants you want, or you'll waste money on unsuitable plants. One novice gardener spent sixty dollars on mums and planted them in a carefully dug round bed underneath an oak tree. She didn't know the flowers needed full sun, and they failed to thrive.

At the library or book store, look for books with detailed descriptions and color photographs of a variety of plants. Rely on catalogs, also. Ask lots of questions of the people at the greenhouse where you plan to buy the plants. Note how well the plants will withstand cold, whether they need sun or shade, the type of soil they prefer, their moisture requirements, and their height and width. Too many people plant a tiny pine tree next to their house only to find that the branches are soon scraping their siding because they planted it too close.

Think of how plants look and evolve through the seasons. Crabapples are beautiful in May, but when they fall, the tiny rolling apples create a real hazard when the trees are near sidewalks and drives. Choose a sterile variety that doesn't produce fruit. Poppies are pretty, too, but their foliage shrivels and dies right after the plant blooms. Plant them with other plants that will cover the brown leaves.

Once you've created a garden design, remember that it will change over the years. A vegetable garden that once barely provided enough for a family with three children will be too much once the children leave home. The gardener who avoided roses because they were too much work might reconsider that decision later on and develop a downright passion for them. But with a general design plan, you're well on your way to the garden of your dreams.

PLANT HARDINESS IN IOWA

Perhaps the biggest challenge Iowa gardeners face is the cold.

We're blessed with fertile soil and few rocks. Our rainfall is adequate, though we often have to supplement it with watering in late summer. Our summers are hot but still cool enough to allow us to grow a wide variety of plants that would die in hotter climates.

The cold, however, is another matter.

Many gardeners choose the most cold-hardy plants by relying on zones designated by the U.S. Department of Agriculture (USDA), based on temperature extremes in different regions. Southern Iowa ended up in Zone 5 and northern Iowa in Zone 4.

That's why, when you're looking at a gardening catalog, it will say something like "hardy in Zones 5 through 9." That means it should have the cold tolerance to grow as far north as Zone 5.

But use zone recommendations loosely—very loosely. Many Zone 5 gardeners find that the only plants that reliably survive Iowa's brutal winters are plants recommended for as far north as Zone 4. Gardeners who really want to make sure that a plant sur-vives all of Iowa's winters purchase only plants hardy all the way up to Zone 3, which runs across northern Minnesota.

The USDA zone map, for example, says Zone 5's minimum air temperature is twenty degrees below zero. Yet in recent years, with record cold snaps in Iowa, temperatures in northern parts of Zone 5 have dipped to thirty below.

Variations in the cold are just as devastating as the deepness of the cold. We can have a week of bitter cold in February followed by two or three warm, springlike days. The warmth sometimes tricks plants into growth, while lots more cold weather is still to come. The change in weather also can cause the ground to heave, sometimes uprooting plants, particularly perennials. This cycle of late winter warmth and cold can be as devastating as the most brutal cold in January.

There are tricks gardeners can use, however, to give plants a better chance of surviving the winter. They won't allow you to grow a Zone 8 plant in Decorah, but they'll help.

A common technique is to drive a shingle or board into the ground on the north side of the plant, though this gives only minimal protection. You can also create a burlap fence around a plant or group of plants. Drive stakes into the ground in a circle or

square around the plant or plants to be protected. Purchase burlap by the yard at a local nursery, and staple it into a fencelike structure around the plants. Then fill in the cylinder created by the burlap with dry leaves. Or wrap the burlap around the plant. Secure it in place by wrapping twine around the plant and tying snugly.

Another way to protect low-growing plants, especially perennials, is to mulch. Mulching provides a blanketing layer of air and organic material that shields roots from temperature extremes. Good mulching materials include straw, leaves shredded by a mower to prevent scattering, shredded bark, and pine needles or boughs. Grass clippings make a great summer mulch laid on the soil, but when put on top of plants for winter protection, they tend to mat and can suffocate the plants underneath.

In late fall, after the ground has frozen hard, apply mulch three or four inches thick. Remove winter mulch from trees or shrubs in very early April. For flower beds containing perennials and bulbs, remove the mulch in late March or so. You can tell that it's time to remove the mulch when plants start to put out new growth underneath.

A trickier but effective way to improve plant hardiness is to study your land for microclimates, that is, tiny climates within your general climate. The best spots to place plants to protect them from the elements is on a south-facing slope. Avoid the bottom of a slope, where cold air will settle, or the top of a hill where they will be exposed to wind. Plant hardiness can also be improved by planting on the south side of a building or evergreen hedge to block the drying winds from the north.

Providing good soil drainage also helps plants survive the winter. When planting, make sure you work in lots of organic matter, such as compost, rotted leaves, or sphagnum peat moss. Dig the bed at least eighteen inches deep. Avoid planting in low-lying areas where water collects.

Fruit trees and other plants susceptible to late spring frost damage should be planted on the north side of a slope. This makes them blossom a little later, protecting them from frosts that might damage early blooms.

Other plants that traditionally aren't very hardy can be grown if you can locate a hardy variety. Not all azaleas will thrive in Iowa, but the "Northern Lights" series will. It can take some searching through specialty catalogs to find these extra-hardy plants, but you will be rewarded with a garden full of your favorite plants.

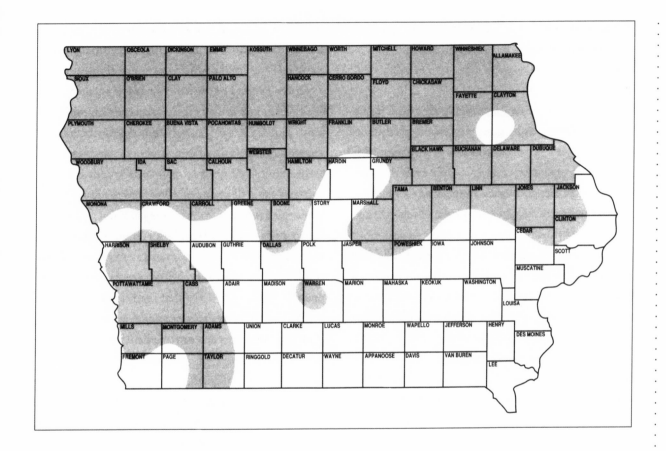

These are the USDA zones for Iowa. Use them in determining whether the plants you buy will survive Iowa's cold winter.

AVERAGE ANNUAL MINIMUM TEMPERATURES

Zone 4   −30° to −20°

Zone 5   −20° to −10°

GARDENING BY MAIL

In Iowa, where specialty nurseries are few and far between, gardening enthusiasts rely on the plethora of mail-order catalogs now available (see pages 136–139). These gardening catalogs supply even the hardest-to-find plants and tools. If you want a heirloom tomato variety or an unusual spading fork, chances are you'll get it only through a catalog. Nurseries do their best to keep as much stock as possible, but they cater to mainstream tastes and needs. That leaves out a lot of interesting plants and gardening supplies. Ordering by mail isn't a perfect process, however. Follow these rules when gardening by mail.

Deal only with reputable companies. It's easy to get inferior plants by mail. If prices look too good to be true, they probably are. Order from companies you or a gardening friend have heard of and have had a good experience with. Not-very-scrupulous suppliers will send you undersized bulbs and plants that die or simply never bloom. Or they'll send you stock in the late fall when it can't be planted.

Compare shipping and handling costs. Some companies charge a lot to ship plants; others ship for no additional charge. Keep that in mind when you order, and don't hesitate to complain if you think shipping and handling charges are too high. Eventually, good companies respond to customer suggestions.

Order early. The earlier you place an order, the more likely you are to get the plants or supplies you want. January is not too early to order for the following spring, especially if you need a large quantity of plant material or unusual plants. If you order early, you may get a discount of 10 percent or more or get bonus plants free.

Neatness counts. Print your order clearly, and make sure you totaled the items correctly. This can save a delay in shipment. Make sure you've included your check if you're using that method of payment.

Use a credit card when practical. It's easier to get a refund or change your order when you use a credit card.

Keep a copy of your order. You may think that you'll always remember precisely how you spent forty dollars on seeds. But in a couple of months, you may well have forgotten whether you got pink or yellow snapdragons or whether you decided on those squash seeds. Photocopy the order if possible. It's also a good way to make sure you receive everything you ordered.

If you're unhappy in any way with your order, call the company. It may suggest how to fix your problem or arrange a return or exchange.

GARDENING RECORDS

Save time, effort, and money without ever getting out of your easy chair: start a garden journal.

Gardeners have a variety of ways of keeping track of their hobby. Some use a notebook. Others keep a file box or make notes on recipe cards. Romantics like a pretty blank book. High-tech gardeners use their personal computers.

These records can be as elaborate or as simple as you'd like, but perhaps the most important thing to keep track of is plants. It might not matter to you at planting time that the annual blue salvia you planted was the "Victoria" variety, but it will in September when that salvia is the glory of your garden. You'll want to be sure to plant it again next year, but you can do that only if you remember its name. And perhaps in June of last year, you saw a glorious iris at a neighbor's garden but can't remember what it is. A journal will remind you.

It is also important to keep a rough gardener's calendar. This helps you plan your garden year after year and prevents gardening problems. In May, you can make a note in your journal that you have too many yellow tulips in the garden and you need to plant more red tulips for contrast by the front door and back by the lilac bushes. That way, come September, you'll actually remember what to plant and where to plant it.

You can also prevent gardening problems with good record keeping. It may be too late to remedy the black spot on your roses this year, but if you make a note of it, next spring you can treat your roses with a fungicide early to prevent the problem. Experienced vegetable gardeners keep track of what they planted where so they can rotate crops.

Gardening records also can keep track of garden plans and designs and gardening expenses, hold your notes on ideal plant varieties, and keep other vital information. Including photographs of your garden will make you view your garden more objectively and give you a visual record from year to year.

One way to create gardening records is to keep them in a three-ring looseleaf notebook. A plastic zip pocket can hold empty seed packets and plant labels. Notebook paper can be used for your garden journal. Paper pockets can hold garden plans sketched out on graph paper and clippings from magazines and newspapers. Use a new notebook each year.

No matter what sort of records you keep, investing time now to record garden information pays rich rewards later.

When cleaning your fireplace, save the ashes to spread on your garden. Potatoes, especially, will benefit from nutrients in the ashes. You can also put the ashes in your compost heap.
ESTER DOCKSTADER,
DES MOINES
GARDEN CLUB

FEBRUARY

FEBRUARY CHECKLIST

🌿 Start leeks from seed the first part of the month. Onions, broccoli, cabbage, cauliflower, and perennial herbs can be started from seed in the middle of the month. These seedlings can be transplanted outdoors in early April, or you can buy established plants later at your local greenhouse.

🌿 Take in lawn mower blades, saws, pruning shears, and other gardening tools for a sharpening. Places that repair lawn mowers or sharpen scissors and knives usually will do this.

🌿 If you have a cold frame, plant radishes, spinach, and lettuce in it late this month.

🌿 Prune most deciduous trees in late February or in March. Wait until July to prune oaks and walnuts to avoid wilt diseases.

🌿 Continue watering amaryllis plants indoors until the flowers fade.

🌿 Wash any pots you plan to use for germinating seeds with hot, soapy water. Rinse well.

🌿 Now, before the spring rush, is a good time to make any trellises, window boxes, or other outdoor structures for your garden.

🌿 Order or purchase devices that allow you to plant early and protect plants from the cold. These include Wall O' Water tepees, hotcaps, cold frames, floating row covers, and plastic mulches that allow you to warm the soil. Many of these allow you to plant vegetables weeks earlier than usual.

🌿 Stop at the library and pick up an armload of gardening books. Larger libraries also have at least a few gardening videos. They give you great ideas for gardening better with less money and effort.

🌱 Set up cold frames, hotbeds, and vegetable beds to be covered with hoops and plastic and other season-extending devices.

🌱 Cut branches from forsythia, redbud, pussy willows, and other spring-blooming shrubs and trees for forcing into bloom indoors. Make two cuts an inch long all the way through the end of the branch to improve its water absorption. Submerge branches entirely in ice-cold water in a tub for a couple of hours. Then stick just the ends in a bucket of cold water about a foot deep for a week in a cool room. Arrange in a vase with water and watch the buds open.

🌱 Check any bulbs forced last fall. When the foliage is about an inch high on larger bulbs, such as tulips, hyacinths, and daffodils, or a half-inch high on smaller bulbs, such as crocuses, dwarf irises, and dwarf daffodils, put them in a very cool place—about fifty degrees—out of direct light for a week. Then place them in a very sunny window. You'll have flowers in a matter of weeks.

Contrary to popular belief, tin cans protect seedlings only from winds. They do not protect from cold. For cold protection for seedlings planted early, remove the lid and cut off the bottom of a plastic milk jug and place over the plant. Remove in mid-May.

BARBARA RUSK,
AMES GARDEN CLUB

Cold-Weather Gardening

With Iowa's cold springs and early autumns, it's important for Iowa gardeners to learn tricks for extending the growing season.

Savvy gardeners create spring on demand with plastic mulches, cold frames, floating row covers, and other materials that warm the soil and create mini-greenhouses. These are the gardeners who have sweet corn and tomatoes weeks before anyone else. They then use the same tricks in fall to continue harvests of fresh vegetables into January.

You, too, can have the earliest—and the latest—harvests on your block. Here's how.

Build a cold frame. This is an indispensable structure for hardening off seedlings, starting small plantings of lettuces and radishes, overwintering marginally hardy plants, and much more. It's so easy and inexpensive to build that every Iowa gardener with even a moderate interest in vegetables and flowers should have one. The sole drawback is that plants can get overheated if you leave the top closed on a sunny day. (See pages 98–99 for more information on cold frames.)

Choose seed and plant varieties carefully. If you want to harvest vegetables early, choose varieties bred to bear early. Some tomatoes bear ninety days from germination, others in as little as sixty-five. If you want to harvest plants into early winter, look for varieties of plants that hold up well to cold. "Rouge d'Hiver," for example, is a red romaine lettuce that can take cold far better than other lettuces. Plant it in August in a cold frame, and you can have fresh lettuce from your garden through Thanksgiving.

Keep track of soil temperatures. With the use of a soil thermometer, you can plant seeds at the earliest possible moment. Some seeds and seedlings thrive in cool soil, while others like warmer soil.

When the soil temperature is fifty degrees, you can transplant seedlings of vegetables that like cool weather, including broccoli, onions, cauliflower, celery, leeks, spinach, cabbage, parsley, perennial herbs, and lettuce. You can start these from seed, or you can buy them established at a nursery.

When the soil temperature has reached sixty-eight degrees, usually in mid-March or so, you can plant peas, lettuce, spinach, turnips, beets, greens, carrots, radishes, and other cool-loving seeds.

When the soil temperature has reached seventy to seventy-five degrees, usually in late May, you can plant seeds such as cucumbers, corn, melons, and squash.

Create plant tunnels. These are a more portable variation on the cold frame and can cover larger areas. Plastic or metal hoops are stuck in the ground and covered with clear plastic that has small vents slashed in it with a sharp knife. The effect is a miniature greenhouse that warms the soil and protects the plants from cold and frost. When the weather warms, the plastic is removed. When late fall comes and frost threatens, plants are again covered to extend the harvest.

These tunnel-like gardens should be erected in late February and early March. Place a series of hoops in a row at four-foot intervals over prepared garden soil. The hoops can be purchased through garden supply stores. They can also be made by inserting flexible plastic tubing or pliable branches into the ground.

Tie the hoops together with lengths of twine to prevent them from flopping over. Cover with clear plastic, and anchor the sides with soil, bricks, or long staples made from old wire coat hangers.

With both plant tunnels and cold frames, as a rule of thumb, you can plant seeds and seedlings outside about four weeks earlier than you could without protection.

Peas, lettuce, spinach, turnips, beets, greens, carrots, radishes, and other cool-loving seeds can be planted in early March in the tunnel or in a cold frame. (Be sure to provide ventilation or lift the frame's lid when temperatures rise, or the plants will get too warm.)

In early April, you can plant warmth-loving seedlings, such as tomatoes, green peppers, melons, squash, and annual herbs like basil.

When the soil temperature has reached seventy to seventy-five degrees, usually in early to mid-May in a cold frame or tunnel, you can plant seeds of cucumbers, corn, melons, and squash in your garden.

Keep the soil moist. You can water by poking a hose right through the tunnel's ventilation slashes.

In mid-April, remove the plastic from the cool-loving plants. Leave the plastic on the warmth-loving plants until mid to late May, when the danger of frost has passed.

In October, when the first frost is near, cover the hoops once again with plastic to keep plants under the hoops warm. The plants listed previously (peas, lettuce, etc.) that like cool weather will survive nicely well past frost with the extra protection. You will be able to harvest your plants for weeks after the first frost.

In the fall, you can cover larger plants, like tomatoes, that don't fit under hoops with floating row cover. It's available under a variety of brand names. This superlight, white fabric cover allows rain and

❧❧ TIP ❧❧

Put two paper coffee filters or a layer of newspaper in the bottom of a pot before filling it with potting soil. It will prevent the soil from washing out.
ROSA CRAWFORD,
KELLOGG GARDEN CLUB

Scatter seeds of poppies or larkspur on the snow in February, and mark with a plant label. As the snow melts, the seeds will settle into the soil and begin growth earlier than usual.

BUENA VIEW
GARDEN CLUB

sun to penetrate but will ward off frost for several weeks.

Use individual cold-protecting devices. You can use smaller devices on individual plants. Wall O' Water tepees are clear-plastic cylinders that encircle a single plant. The sides are filled with water, which collects heat during the day. They work well on tomatoes, green peppers, and eggplants.

To use, in mid-March fill the tepees with water. Put them in place to warm the soil where you'll be planting the seedlings about three days before planting. Plant the seedling and water it. Remove the tepees in mid-May.

If you want only a couple weeks' jump on the growing season, you can plant the cool-loving seedlings the first week of April and keep them covered with a cloche, made by cutting the bottom out of a milk jug with its cap removed. You can plant warmth-loving seedlings the first week of May and cover with cloches.

You must remove the cloches each day (unless it's a particularly cold day) to allow enough sunlight for the plants. Plants can get too warm under these cloches on sunny days.

Plant for fall, too. In late July or early August, plant seeds for fall and winter harvests. Quick-growing plants, such as lettuces, spinaches, and kale, work well. Unlike spring plantings, you don't have to protect these seedlings from the cold. But you do need to be diligent in keeping them well watered during the often-dry days of high summer.

In late September, when the first frost threatens, cover lettuces, spinaches, and other vegetables susceptible to frost with the vented plastic or superlight floating row cover. The plants won't grow any more, but they'll stay in good shape for another month or so as if they were in a giant refrigerator. Simply lift the row cover to harvest.

In early October, cover root vegetables, such as rutabaga, turnips, celeriac, carrots, leeks, and others, with a layer of straw about six inches thick. This will prevent the ground from freezing. Leave the kale and Brussels sprouts as they are—a light frost improves their flavor. Mark the plants with stakes that protrude three or four feet above the ground. Label the stakes. In the winter, even after snow covers the ground, you will be able to dig through the snow, straw, and soil to harvest the vegetables beneath.

STARTING PLANTS FROM SEEDS

Too many people buy seeds, plant them indoors, and wait—and wait—for something to happen. Nothing does, so they dump the whole mess into the backyard and give up.

That's a pity. Like baking bread, growing plants from seed takes a knack, but it's not a complicated process. The trick is to start small and choose very easy seeds, such as marigolds or tomatoes. Once you've mastered these, move on to something more challenging.

Perennials are especially worth starting from seed because you save big bucks. Perennials that can cost five dollars each as established plants cost just pennies each when started from seed. Having good instructions helps. When choosing seed, it pays to order from really good catalogs. They give detailed planting instructions and sometimes even free booklets with each order. They also designate which seeds are easiest to grow.

Expect limited success (as in perhaps just 25 percent of your seeds germinating) the first year, and be prepared to learn from your mistakes. Each year you'll learn more until eventually you'll be able to grow rather difficult plants from seed.

As a rule of thumb, here's how to start most plants from seed.

Choose a container with drainage holes. Containers can be the cell packs in which you buy annuals, pots, egg cartons, or just about anything else that has drainage holes. The little clear-plastic boxes with snap-on tops that lettuce is sold in are excellent. They even have ventilation and drainage holes. Wash any container with hot, soapy water and rinse well to kill harmful organisms.

Don't use regular garden soil. Instead, use one of the specially formulated sterile growing mediums made just for seedlings. If the seeds need to be covered, use vermiculite.

Follow seed packet directions absolutely to the letter. If the directions say to leave the seeds uncovered, do so. If they say to cover the seeds, cover them with vermiculite to the depth specified. Its light color makes it easy to see what you covered, and it holds water in such a way to prevent disease in new seedlings.

Cover with plastic wrap, a pane of glass, or other clear material. This cuts down on drafts, conserves moisture, and creates a cozy miniature greenhouse for the seedlings.

Water seeds carefully. Instead of pouring water

These plants are especially easy to start indoors from seed.

ANNUALS	PERENNIALS AND BIENNIALS
Bachelor's-buttons	Campanula
Cosmos	Coreopsis
Impatiens	Digitalis
Larkspur	Goldenrod
Marigolds	Hollyhocks
Pansies	Liatris
Petunias	Monarda
Salvia	Phlox
Snapdragons	Purple
Sunflowers	coneflower
Sweet pea	Statice
Violas	Yarrow
Zinnias	

These plants are especially easy to start indoors from seed.

VEGETABLES AND EDIBLE PLANTS
Basil
Broccoli
Brussels sprouts
Cauliflower
Cilantro
Green peppers
Herbs
Hot peppers
Leeks
Lettuce
Onions
Parsley
Spinach

over the soil, which would wash out the seeds, set the container in a pan of warm water. Let the water wick up through the soil until the top of the soil is just moist. You can also water the seeds by dribbling water on slowly with your hand. A bulb sprinkler, available through Park's Seed Company (see page 137), costs only a few dollars and is excellent for this type of watering.

Put the seeds in an area that is the temperature indicated on the seed package. Some plants like to germinate at seventy degrees. Others want it as cool as fifty-five degrees. Using a room thermometer, find warm and cool spots around your house. Leave the containers in the appropriate spot until the seeds germinate, usually in a week or two.

Don't be disappointed if not all the seeds germinate. Seldom does a gardener get 100 percent germination. The more experienced you get in growing plants from seeds, however, the better germination rates you will get.

As soon as the seeds begin to germinate, remove the plastic or glass from the top to allow air to circulate. Put them in the brightest spot you can manage. A south-facing window is good. If you have many seedlings, set up a shop light or one of the new high-intensity plant lights in your basement. Keep the light no more than six inches above the seedlings. Or try one of the new superbright grow lights available through mail-order catalogs such as Worm's Way Garden Supply (see page 139). Used by hydroponics enthusiasts, they're far brighter than conventional grow lights.

Keep the soil moist but not too damp. If the soil is soggy, plants will "damp off," that is, rot at soil level. If they dry out at all, the delicate seedlings will die.

Give the seedlings direct sunlight as soon as possible. On sunny days in late March or April, a cold frame is ideal for providing direct sun without exposing seedlings to cold temperatures. You can even cobble together a temporary cold frame by propping a storm window against a south-facing building. Put the seedlings underneath, and close the ends with scrap lumber held in place with bricks. Take plants inside at night.

In mid-May, move your seedlings permanently outdoors. If they haven't been in a cold frame, "harden off" seedlings by exposing them to the outdoors for a few hours at a time, gradually increasing the time over a period of three or four days. Then plant them in a well-prepared bed with good soil. Give them plenty of room so established plants don't crowd them. Keep well watered for the first two weeks.

BASIC TOOLS

There's a myth that gardeners need lots of specialized tools and expensive gadgets. Nothing could be further from the truth. Farmers in ancient times worked with little more than pointed sticks. Today, all you really need to get started in gardening are five tools: a mower, a hose, a spade, a sprinkler, and a leaf rake. There are, of course, a lot of other tools that make your gardening chores much easier, but with these five starter tools you will be on your way.

When purchasing garden tools, expensive doesn't always mean better, but dirt-cheap tools usually have to be replaced after a few seasons. Better to shop at a reputable hardware store or order through a good-quality mail-order catalog. (Garage sales also turn up some great bargains.) You don't need beautifully crafted, English-made tools, but look for sturdy, rust-proof materials and solid construction. Garden tools take a lot of abuse.

An important note: never leave tools outside for more than a few hours. Dew, rain, sun, and other elements will destroy your investment.

Although you may need a garden tool right away, when possible, wait until August and September to buy tools. That's when hardware stores put them on clearance.

Here are some of the basic garden tools you will need.

Mower. Although this is probably the most expensive garden tool you'll buy, a mower is a must for lawns. If you have a small, flat lawn, you can use an old-fashioned reel mower. Otherwise, you'll probably need a power mower. A bag for collecting grass clippings saves time and creates perfect composting material. Mulching mowers chop clippings finely and put them back on the lawn, where they feed the grass and prevent weeds. You can often buy good-quality second-hand power mowers for far less money than new ones. Check with a local mower dealer.

Hose. Buy a medium- to high-quality hose that's long enough to reach even the farthermost parts of your yard. Old hoses can be repaired for pennies with fitting replacements.

Spade. This is essential for digging flower beds, turning over vegetable gardens, planting trees or shrubs, and a number of other uses. Some gardeners prefer spades with round tips over square tips and vice versa. Make sure the handle is a comfortable length.

Sprinkler. There are many types on the market, but look for an all-metal model. They're more durable than plastic sprinklers. Some sprinklers cover

very large areas, and others are better suited to smaller lawns and gardens.

Leaf rake. Use this for removing fall leaves, grass clippings, and other debris from your garden.

Eventually, add the following garden tools.

Hand trowel. This is used for everything from planting seedlings to scooping potting soil to cultivating the soil around plants and removing weeds.

Large watering can. Buy the largest one you can carry comfortably when full. This is good for watering potted plants or small plantings after you've transplanted them. This also is good for mixing fertilizers or other liquid soil amendments. The big plastic cans are just as good as those expensive ones made from brass and galvanized steel.

Ground rake. This heavy metal rake can smooth out beds and gardens after you turn them over. It's also useful in cleaning up garden debris.

Five-gallon bucket. These are often free from restaurants and supermarkets, or you can buy them at farm supply stores. Good for mixing soil, hauling small loads around the yard, harvesting fruits and vegetables, washing tools, watering, collecting weeds, and a million other uses.

Hoe. This is good for weeding between plants and making planting rows. There are dozens of different

types of hoes, but the plain, flat-edged broad garden hoe is the most versatile.

Hand pruning shears. Shears are used for trimming small branches from trees and shrubs. They are also good for cutting woody weeds or plants. Buy the bypass kind that cut like scissors. The shears with an anvil-like mechanism crush rather than cut plants and should be avoided.

Drop spreader or hose spray attachment. The drop spreader is used to apply dry fertilizer and weed killers quickly and evenly. Use carefully and read directions for both the spreader and the chemicals you buy. The hose spray attachment is used for the same purpose but is filled with chemical mixtures and is attached to a garden hose. Water flowing through the hose creates enough suction to withdraw some of the chemical, which is sprayed from the container. Follow directions carefully.

Hand saw. There are dozens of different pruning saws. A trip to the hardware store and a conversation with a knowledgeable clerk will get you a good general-purpose saw.

MARCH

March Checklist

🌿 Most trees, shrubs, and berries can be pruned now. (See pages 31–32 for more information.) These include grapevines, raspberries, currants, gooseberries, fruit trees, and most shade trees.

🌿 Spray fruit trees with dormant oil to prevent scale insects and spider mites later. Apply when temperature is above forty degrees.

🌿 Begin planting trees and shrubs.

🌿 Start spring cleanup. Take advantage of this month's occasional pleasant days to rake leaves that have accumulated over the winter and to pick up trash and broken limbs, etc.

🌿 Gradually remove winter protection from roses but do not remove the mounded dirt around them yet. Gradually uncover climbing roses you have removed from their trellises and buried with soil.

🌿 Although you can buy established seedlings later on, if you want you can start onions, leeks, broccoli, cabbage, and cauliflower from seed early in the month. Mid-month, plant peppers, eggplant, and parsley from seed. Also plant cool-loving bedding plants, such as pansies, godetias, snapdragons, and violas. At the end of the month, plant tomato seeds, or wait until early April.

🌿 Don't remove mulch from strawberries and other perennials too early. To determine when to remove mulch, gently rake away part of the mulch to examine plants underneath. If you can see new, green growth, it's time to remove the mulch. Add old mulch to the compost heap.

Be careful about working soil in your garden if it's wet. Spading wet soil will make it dry in large, hard clumps and ruin the texture of the soil.

Visit greenhouses and other plant outlets to price plants. Take note of what's available and how much items cost. Prices can vary considerably even when quality might not.

If you have a cold frame (see pages 98–99), plant lettuce, spinach, and radishes now for spring salads in a couple of months.

Save the oil drained from your car and mix it with sand in a box or pail. When you're through with a garden tool, such as a spade, plunge it into the oiled sand to clean and oil it in one operation.

WILMA LESAN,

AMES GARDEN CLUB

PREPARING THE SOIL

If experienced gardeners could tell beginners just one thing, they'd put it in a flashing neon sign and post it high for everyone to see. It's this: prepare your soil well.

It's hard to emphasize enough good soil preparation, but it's one of the most neglected garden practices around. Sure, you can get something to grow in even the worst soil. But if you want a good garden that takes little watering, repels disease and insects naturally, and produces well, work on the soil.

Before you take the spade to the earth, however, give time and thought to making it the absolutely best piece of land that you can. For most purposes, your goal is to get it as close to potting soil as possible—crumbly, black, rich.

It's a good idea to test your soil's pH level, a measurement of its acidity or alkalinity. Most garden plants thrive on a pH of 6 to 7, a fairly neutral soil. If the pH level is alkaline (above pH 7), the soil may need sulfur. If the soil's pH is too low (below 6), it's acidic and needs lime. (Contrary to folk wisdom, don't add lime unless you know your soil is acidic and needs it. Lime raises the pH of the soil, so adding it automatically may throw off the pH of the soil.) Although Iowa's soil has a reputation for being neutral, it ranges anywhere from 5.5 to 8 on the pH scale, a substantial difference.

Some plants actually like pH levels that aren't often found in Iowa. Rhododendrons and lupines, for example, like acidic soil. Knowing if you have very acidic or very alkaline soil can guide your choice of plants.

PH levels may vary from spot to spot in your yard. The leaves of oak trees, for example, break down and acidify the soil beneath.

You can buy soil-testing kits that cost quite a bit, but the Iowa State University Soil Testing Laboratory will test your soil for just a few dollars. The laboratory also gauges phosphorous and potassium levels. The extension service will also test for other soil elements and soil texture for an additional fee. Contact your local county extension service for more information (see pages 145–148).

After checking the soil's pH, check the texture of your soil. Is it full of reddish or yellowish clay? Does it hold its shape in a tight ball when a handful is squeezed? Or is it sandy, that is, very crumbly and water runs through it easily? If you're lucky, it's neither. Instead it's loam—black, crumbly, and forming a very loose ball when you squeeze it.

If you have sandy soil, be prepared to add two or three inches of sphagnum peat moss (not the stuff labeled simply "peat") and compost, available at garden centers. If it's full of clay, sprinkle gypsum on the soil according to instructions on the bag and work in two or three inches of sharp sand.

To prepare soil, first deal with any weeds or sod at the site. This can be done with a spade, digging up squares of turf that can be planted elsewhere in your yard. If the sod is sparse, simply work it into the soil. It will break down and add organic matter. (An extremely easy way to create a flower or vegetable bed is simply to cover the area with two or three layers of newspaper. Cover the paper with sand, compost, or black topsoil. Wait from between three to six weeks— or over the winter—while the grass dies and the paper breaks down. Then turn over the whole area with a spade.)

To any bed, add about three inches of organic material. Though it is a hassle and can be rather expensive (if you don't have lots of compost and other materials on hand), this is critical for successful gardening. You will save the money invested in organic material many times over by not having to buy bug sprays or replacing sick plants.

Organic matter can be one of several things or a mixture of several, including sphagnum peat moss, compost, well-rotted manure (fresh manure will burn plants unless you let the soil lie fallow for at least a month), and chopped and partly decayed leaves.

Now the backbreaking part: turning over the soil. If you can bear it, use a spading fork or spade and do it by hand. Powered tilling machines don't go deeply enough for this initial working of the soil.

Dig the soil to a depth of about eighteen inches. That might seem awfully deep when digging a large bed, but it is far better to prepare only a little piece of land well than a large piece of land badly. Rake the soil smooth with a ground rake. You're ready to plant.

TIP

When buying bedding plants, choose those that aren't in bloom. If they already have bloomed, pinch off the blooms when you plant them. Your plant will get established faster, and you will have a bushier plant.

AGNES KOZISEK,

VENTURA

GARDEN CLUB

VEGETABLE GARDENING

There is nothing as rewarding as strolling into your vegetable patch and picking the reddest, ripest tomato you've ever seen or plucking tender yellow ears of sweet corn from their stalks and racing to the kitchen where a large pot of boiling water waits. First-time vegetable gardeners often begin dreaming of these treats in winter, storm their local garden centers in spring, and go berserk. They plant twelve tomato plants, row upon row of corn, zucchini (even though they hate it), green peppers, cabbages, broccoli, cauliflower, peas, lettuce, spinach, Brussels sprouts, kohlrabi, rutabaga, and celeriac.

That's a mistake. Beginning gardeners should grow no more than a half-dozen or so vegetables their first year. This assures that they won't be overwhelmed with weeds in July and with produce in August. It also assures that they won't break their backs digging the garden and that they'll be able to eat most of what they grow.

Beginning gardeners usually should choose from among the following garden plants: tomatoes, peas, carrots, radishes, lettuces, spinach, broccoli, green peppers, green beans, ever-bearing strawberries, squash, and cucumbers. Corn is fine as long as you have enough space.

First-time vegetable plots seldom should be larger than one hundred square feet, unless you have a large family or plan on doing a lot of canning and freezing. Most beginning gardeners find their garden is too large, not too small.

With vegetable gardens, as in real estate, location is everything. Many a gardener has started a vegetable garden in a too-shady spot, only to be disappointed with spindly plants riddled with disease. Or maybe the garden was far from the house, where no one ever looked at it, and subsequently, no one ever tended it.

The ideal site for a vegetable garden is a very sunny spot that gets at least six hours of full sun, that is, six hours of sun with absolutely no shadows. It's close enough to the kitchen door to allow the cook a quick dash to the garden for a couple of fresh tomatoes. It's in a spot where it's regularly seen, not tucked behind a garage in a spot where no one would otherwise visit.

Don't rule out the middle of your backyard as a possible location. When laid out in attractive geometric patterns, a vegetable garden is every bit as attractive as an herb garden.

If possible, the site should be level to facilitate easy tilling and to prevent soil erosion. However, don't rule out a steep slope, especially if a slope faces south.

With terraces, it can make an ideal garden site with excellent drainage.

The quality of the soil should be taken into consideration. Take a spade and dig up a little soil to a depth of about twelve to eighteen inches. If it's black and crumbly, you probably have excellent soil. If it's yellowish and forms a sticky ball in your hand, it has a high clay content and is going to need some work (see page 86 for instructions on improving soil). If it's very gritty and crumbly, it's sandy and will also need improvement.

To check out a possible site, on a day after the ground has thawed (early April or so), dig a hole eighteen inches deep and about a foot wide. Fill it with water. If the water is still standing after a day or two, the ground doesn't drain well, and you should find a different site.

If you're tight on space, think creatively in finding a site. Consider renting part of a public garden, an unused lot owned by the city, or land along railroad tracks.

And don't toss out your front yard or flower beds as a possibility for at least some edible plants. Rhubarb, strawberries, pole beans, lettuces, potatoes, grapes, and even corn are as beautiful as they are edible.

Keep containers in mind. You can raise an amazing number of tomatoes and peppers in a small spot by the back door with a few herbs in pots. When creating a container vegetable garden, look for varieties that are recommended specifically for containers.

In creating a vegetable garden, prepare the soil well (see pages 26–27). Good soil solves many other problems later on. Plants will be more disease resistant, and soil will drain well during wet spells and retain moisture during dry spells. Good soil is a joy to plant in and is easier on the back.

There are a number of ways to plant your garden. Our grandparents used to plant each variety in a single long row across their gardens. Since then, a number of new planting techniques have evolved, such as grouping plants in square patches (often called "square-foot gardening"), growing plants in raised beds, vertical gardening, organic gardening, and low-maintenance gardening.

Beginning gardeners should simply do whatever makes sense for them, though a simple, old-fashioned plan for a vegetable garden that draws on several of the preceding techniques is included here. Intermediate gardeners may want to check out or purchase books on the gardening methods that interest them.

Once your vegetables are planted, mulch to keep down the weeds and to conserve moisture. Straw, hay, wood chips, and pine needles work well. So do grass clippings that have not been treated with herbicides.

TREES AND SHRUBS FOR IOWA

Plant the wrong tree or shrub badly, and you'll regret it for a long time.

Among the toughest decisions you'll have as a gardener is which trees and shrubs to plant where and which trees and shrubs to take out or severely alter. These are the giants of your garden, so they're important.

If you're planting a tree or shrub, do your research first. Check the list of some of the top trees and shrubs for Iowa on pages 130–132. Pore through books from the library, or at least check the plant list in the back of this book. Consult your local county extension agent (see pages 144–148). Or find and ask questions of someone who seems to know something at the garden center.

To select a tree or shrub, make a list of the characteristics you want in the plant. Do you want it for shade or spring blooms? Do you want your own cherries? Do you yearn for bright fall color? How large should it be? What sort of growing conditions will it have? How much space? Then make another list of characteristics you don't want, like messy fruit, aggressive root systems, or large size.

This list in hand, call or visit local nurseries. Ask lots of questions about the plant's ideal growing conditions and its advantages and disadvantages. Be prepared to order a special variety, if necessary. Compare prices for different sizes of the same plant. And since this is Iowa, always ask: how hardy is it?

All this might be work, but remember that a tree or shrub is something you're likely to live with for years. Choose something you'll like.

Plant bare-root trees and shrubs as early as March and as late as May. You can plant potted or balled-and-burlapped shrubs in September, but you'll have slightly more risk of winter damage or kill.

Prepare the soil well, digging a hole about twice the size you need to comfortably fit in the plant's roots. Work a little compost into the hole. If the plant is bare-root, soak it overnight in water and plant. If the plant is in a container or balled-and-burlapped, remove the container or fabric and plant it at the same depth it was in the container or ball.

Water well and mulch with shredded bark, grass clippings, or other organic matter. Extend the mulch out a couple of feet or more from the trunk or stem. This will protect the plant from lawn mower damage, keep down competing weeds, and conserve moisture. Keep the plant well watered for the rest of the season, but don't overwater.

PRUNING BASICS

Pruning can be a perplexing task. When is the right time to prune? Which branches need pruning? What are the right tools to use?

Too few gardeners know the basics of pruning. As a result, they end up giving their most prized trees and shrubs pruning jobs that look like bad haircuts.

Don't assume that you must prune each year. While many people prune evergreens into tight little balls or cones, evergreens often look better (and require less maintenance) when allowed to assume their natural shapes. The same holds true of forsythias, lilacs, spirea, and many of our other favorite shrubs.

You should prune at least occasionally, though, for several reasons. Many shrubs and evergreen trees, especially those planted in hedges, will simply get too big if you don't trim them. And young trees for the first several years of their lives need diligent pruning to make sure they grow into shapely, attractive trees. Many favorites, such as lilacs and crabapples, send up suckers or shoots at the base of the plant that must be removed to keep the plants' shape and maximum bloom. And there are often dead or broken branches that must be removed.

The trickiest part of pruning is deciding what to cut. But if you follow this cardinal rule of pruning, you shouldn't do much harm: go slowly and step back to check your work often.

Proceed with caution. While just about everyone can prune shrubs, be careful in cutting large tree limbs more than a few inches in diameter, cutting limbs while standing on top of a high ladder, or cutting limbs near power lines. These jobs may well best be left to a professional or your local utility service.

If you're going to hire a professional, hire someone who has extensive experience, has an eye for well-shaped plants, is knowledgeable about tree varieties, and has good references. Just because a person is willing to take money for pruning doesn't mean the person has much skill. Many a prized tree or shrub has been ruined by someone with too much enthusiasm and a chain saw.

What do you prune and when? As a rule, most trees and shrubs should be pruned in late February or in March. These include evergreens, most deciduous trees and bushes, grapes, berries, and fruit trees. That's when the plants are just starting to send out new growth, so you can tell what's thriving and what's not and then remove any dead limbs or branches. Also, the plants aren't yet so cluttered with foliage that you can't see their "bones," their general shape.

When pruning, keep an eye out for branches that rub each other or will come close to it. Prune the plant to eliminate the problem.

Wait until summer to prune oaks and walnuts to avoid disease and wilt. Prune spring-blooming shrubs after they're done blooming. These include lilacs, forsythias, and ornamental crabapples.

Contrary to folk wisdom, don't paint wounds with tree paint. Don't fill large cavities with concrete. And don't ever, ever "top" a tree, that is, trim the top. If you must trim a tree to prevent it from growing taller, keep the tree's general form. Cut each branch back to a crotch in the tree.

Be careful when trimming evergreens. Many people cut back evergreens severely, not realizing that many types only have new growth on the exterior of the plant. Cutting back past the layer of green growth leaves the unattractive brown needles and ruins the entire plant. Trim evergreens lightly, and check with your local nursery or a horticulturist on the proper way to trim your particular variety.

Whenever possible, use the proper tools. A pruning saw, loppers, and a good all-purpose pair of hand pruning shears can save you aching arms and hours of work. Keep them razor sharp, taking them in for a sharpening at least once a year. Oil them lightly periodically to prevent rust. With a little knowledge and the right tools, you'll be well on your way to a more attractive landscape.

APRIL

APRIL CHECKLIST

🌿 If you choose to use lawn chemicals, apply crabgrass preventer to the lawn. Also fertilize your lawn. You can purchase a "weed and feed" combination at your local garden center. Follow package directions exactly. An organic alternative is to use the natural lawn-care products now available, including an Iowa State University–developed weed killer made from corn, A-Maizing Lawn, available through Gardens Alive! (See page 137 for ordering information.)

🌿 April is a good time to have plugs of soil taken out of your lawn to aerate it. Your lawn should be aerated once every two or three years to alleviate compaction. You can also do this in the fall.

🌿 Dig new flower beds and gardens when weather permits. Be careful about digging and working the soil when it's wet. You will end up with large clods that dry into rock-hard clumps.

🌿 Rake up dead twigs, grass, and any trash that have accumulated in your yard over the winter.

🌿 Bring out pots and other containers this month. Plant pansies, which won't mind the cold much, or go ahead and plant other annuals in pots or window boxes late in the month. If frost threatens, throw a sheet over them or bring indoors for protection.

🌿 When turning over your vegetable garden, first spread compost or other organic matter to a depth of about one inch. Till or otherwise work into the top few inches of soil. Done each spring, this greatly improves the quality of your soil. As an alternative, you can work in a slow-release fertilizer instead of the compost, but inorganic fertilizers do nothing to improve the texture of the soil, which is critical to maintaining healthy plants.

In early April, start plants indoors from seeds to set out unprotected in mid-May. These include tomatoes, peppers, marigolds, snapdragons, petunias, and other bedding plants. If you use frost-protective devices, such as Wall O' Water, tepees, floating row covers, or cold frames, you can set out your tomatoes, peppers, and other heat-loving plants mid-month.

Plant nearly any trees and shrubs now.

Plant seedlings of broccoli, cauliflower, cabbage, Brussels sprouts, leeks, parsnips, lettuces, spinach, chives, tarragon, parsley, sage, thyme, oregano, other perennial herbs, and onion sets outdoors mid-month. You can also plant cool-loving flowers outside mid-month, including pansies, Iceland poppies, violas, primulas, English daisies, and godetias.

As soon as you can work the ground, plant directly in the soil seeds of peas, carrots, radishes, turnips, beets, greens, endive, Swiss chard, and other cool-loving plants. Seeds of corn and other plants should wait until the soil is warmer.

Plant small amounts of radishes, spinach, lettuce, and other quick-growing, cool-loving plants every two weeks until hot weather strikes in June. This will give you a slow, steady harvest instead of bushels of produce all at once.

Plant rhubarb, strawberries, raspberries, and asparagus, which are perennials, now.

Plant certified potato seed pieces. Good Friday is the traditional planting date in Iowa.

Consider putting a fence of some sort around the garden to keep out rabbits. A two-foot-tall chicken wire fence works well. Bury the fencing an inch or two beneath the soil, and bend it outward to prevent burrowing. Although there is little if any scientific evidence that this works, some people swear by putting clumps of human hair (available from your local hairdresser) in the feet of panty hose and staking them to the ground to drive away rabbits. Others sprinkle bloodmeal on the ground. Both need to be reapplied after a rain.

Divide most perennial flowers now. Many perennials should be divided every three or four years. Plants need to be divided when they start to have fewer blooms each year, develop a dead spot in the middle of the clump of stems, or otherwise seem crowded. To divide, dig up the entire plant. Break the roots into several clumps with your hands or a spading fork. Replant the clumps, leaving twelve to eighteen inches between them.

Remove mulch from strawberries when 25 percent of the plants show new growth as yellow leaves. This is usually around April 13 in southern Iowa, April 20 in central Iowa, and April 27 in northern Iowa.

When digging out dandelions, get the top two inches of taproot in order to kill the plant. If you choose to use a herbicide to get rid of dandelions, wait until fall.

Prune roses when their buds just begin to swell and you can tell what wood is dead. Cut out any dead wood. Plant bare-root roses later in the month. Soil mounded around the bases of established roses can be removed in early April by gently hosing or gently scraping with a trowel. Climbing roses can be uncovered in early April and reattached to their supports. Strips of panty hose work well as ties.

Work garden sulfur, peat moss, or Miracid into the soil around acid-loving plants, including rhododendrons and azaleas, hollies, blueberries, and lupines.

After daffodils, tulips, and other bulbs bloom, don't be tempted to trim off the dying foliage. The plants need it to rejuvenate for next spring's bloom. Completely yellow or brown foliage should be removed only after it pulls off with little resistance.

Control ground ivy, also known as creeping charlie and creeping jenny. Though fall is the best time to apply a herbicide to control this weed, you can apply products that contain at least two of the following herbicides: 2,4-D, MCPP, or dicamba. An organic alternative is pulling up or digging out creeping charlie, but it reestablishes itself very easily.

Stay on top of weeding chores, but be careful. Small, hard-to-identify flower seedlings often are lost along with the weeds.

If you wrapped the trunks of tender trees last fall, remove the wrap now.

If you want to get a head start on planting, plant tomatoes and green pepper seedlings outdoors now using Wall O' Water tepees. You can also plant under plastic-covered hoops (see page 17) for an early start.

SHOPPING FOR PLANTS

In a perfect world, garden budgets would not exist. You and your Visa card would sweep merrily through the greenhouse, looking at nary a price tag and buying fifty of this and three dozen of that.

But plants cost money, sometimes lots of money. Resist the urge to buy all plants in sight. A single "Hicksii" yew (which a nursery salesperson once described as "the Cadillac of evergreens") can set you back eighty dollars for what is really just a plain old bush. If you buy a smaller "Hicksii" yew at a discount store, you may end up paying just ten dollars. What can save you and your credit card bill is comparison shopping.

The last week of April is a good time to walk through the greenhouses and garden centers in your area with notebook in hand. Make a note of the cost of the plants you want. Depending on how many and what plants you're buying, the savings may be in the triple digits. If you're planting a hedge, a windbreak, or a large perennial border, comparison shopping can save you hundreds of dollars.

When shopping around, check how many plants are in a cell pack, those little plastic pots that have three, four, or even as many as eight plants in individual cells connected together at their rims. A cell pack with six seedlings retailing for a dollar is a better value than one with three plants selling for seventy-five cents.

Reputable greenhouses and nurseries almost always have top-quality stock and have it for a long time. They also usually have fairly good plant selection. They have ample staff to answer gardening questions. And they often offer guarantees on trees and shrubs. But none of that is free. You pay for it at the checkout counter.

But don't rule out the plants you see at discount stores or even the ones marked half off at the supermarket. If they appear to be green, stocky, vigorous, and otherwise healthy, buy them. Do not, however, buy plants that are wilted or leggy or appear to have any sort of disease or insect infestation. They're a waste of money and time, especially with annuals. And use a grain of salt in heeding the advice of the staff at such places. Unless they've had special training, they're likely to be relying on folk wisdom and their own, often very limited, gardening experience.

Check if a plant is rootbound. If it has white roots coming out of the bottom hole, it will take longer to get established than a plant whose roots aren't as crowded.

Believe it or not, whenever possible you should also purchase plants not yet in bloom. These plants have focused their energy on root and foliage growth, which at this point is more important than flowers. It's tough to resist colorful plants, but you'll be spending your money more wisely.

Smaller plants are usually a better value than larger plants, especially if you're buying trees and shrubs. Some studies have shown that when a small tree and large tree are planted together, the small tree quickly catches up to the size of the larger tree, even though larger trees usually cost substantially more.

The same is true of perennials. Smaller plants usually catch up with larger plants in just one year.

Try growing your potatoes on top of the ground under a cover of straw a few feet deep. This way, you can rob the hill all summer long for new potatoes, and the plants keep growing.
GLORIA BAKER,
BLUE WATER
GARDEN CLUB,
SPIRIT LAKE

Best Perennials for Iowa

For good reason, perennials' popularity has exploded. These hardy plants come back year after year, generally need less water than annuals, and add color and greenery wherever they're planted.

But perennials must be chosen carefully, with climate in mind. In Iowa, with its extremes of wet and dry, winds and severe winter, gardeners must be fairly selective to ensure that their plants will be around for years to come.

An excellent—and cheap—way to acquire perennials is to get them from your friends, family, and neighbors. Phlox, daylilies, daisies, columbine, coreopsis, larkspur, irises, and other perennials thrive here, and the people who grow them usually are more than happy to give up a plant start or two to those who vocally admire their gardens.

These are plants that have withstood the test of time and neglect. If a perennial is growing all around your neighborhood, you know that it's easy to grow. If you see a flower that thrives even around deserted farmhouses, you know it's truly a plant to last the ages.

You can also find plants that survive in Iowa at local plant sales, held as fund-raisers by local garden clubs or by avid gardeners in need of money to support their plant habit. The plants they're selling are usually propagated from their own gardens, so you know they'll probably do well in yours.

But there's a disease risk in getting plants from amateurs. Plants that have been grown in a hodge-podge of conditions might be carrying viruses or harboring insects that you'll introduce into your garden.

When selecting a perennial, besides the usual considerations of its preference for sun or shade, a wet spot or a dry spot, etc., you must also give utmost consideration to its size, blooming period, foliage, color, growth habit, and relationship to nearby plants.

Tall perennials—such as foxglove, delphinium, loosestrife, and hollyhock—belong in the back of flower beds and gardens. Medium-height flowers—such as mums, daisies, yarrow, and columbine—go in the middle. Low and creeping plants—such as perennial alyssum and snow-in-summer—should be planted in the front where they won't be hidden.

Also consider a plant's blooming period. Coreopsis will bloom for nearly two months, while Oriental poppies look good for perhaps a week.

Oriental poppies are also a good example of why it's important to consider a plant's foliage. Their leaves turn brown and withered as soon as the plants finish their brief bloom. Daylilies, on the other hand, have graceful, grasslike leaves that are attractive from the moment they emerge from the soil in early spring until a hard frost kills them in late fall.

Color also is critical. The orange of a butterfly milkweed might well clash with the softer pink of some statices, but it can be the perfect complement to bright blue flowers.

Keep in mind background color, too. White flowers planted against the white side of a house, for example, are unlikely to show up well, while the deep green of an evergreen hedge is often a perfect foil for most perennials.

A perennial's growth habit shouldn't be overlooked. A spreading plant, such as hardy geranium, is a poor choice for a narrow flower bed that abuts the high, blank side of a house. Delphiniums, lupines, heliopsis, pampas grass, or other tall, narrow plants are probably a better selection. Find out whether the plant is invasive or not. Lily-of-the-valley is fragrant and wonderful for cutting, but it can take over a shady area in which it is planted.

Also consider how a perennial will relate to the plants around it. The sharp blades of irises and the orchidlike shape of their flowers are a good contrast to the bushy, round shape of peony foliage and its

cabbage, roselike flowers. Columbine and lady's-mantle are excellent planted on top of or next to tulip bulbs. Their foliage starts growing rapidly just about the time the tulips are done blooming, covering the tulips' browning foliage.

These rules of thumb apply to more than just perennials. You can use them for just about any type of plant, from a towering, regal shade tree to a small and humble annual.

Good soil preparation is critical for a perennial bed or border. Vegetable gardens and annuals are torn out each fall, giving gardeners who are a little lazy a second shot at improving the soil. But perennials are there for years, and there are few second chances. Prepare the soil well the first time (see pages 19–20).

Pamper perennials their first year. Monitor their water carefully, being sure to give them at least an inch of water a week. Water occasionally and well rather than often and lightly. Most perennials prefer deep waterings.

Taller plants, such as digitalis and delphiniums, will need staking. You can buy a variety of professional stakes at the greenhouse or fashion your own out of wooden laths or even tall sticks. Tie the plants gently to the stakes with strips of old panty hose or strips of neutral-colored rags. String or wire can cut into the stems.

Plant radish seeds in with slower germinating seeds, such as carrots or beets. The radishes germinate much earlier, marking the rows. After the radishes mature and are harvested, the slower growing vegetables have room to grow.

JOAN HAUB,
BOONE GARDEN CLUB

Bushy plants—such as some daisies, peonies, and other plants prone to flopping—benefit from circular wire supports. You can use the supports designed for tomatoes, or you can buy other specially designed supports at your greenhouse or through catalogs.

After the first hard frost, cut back plants with pruning shears to about one or two inches. Throw undiseased plant refuse on the compost heap. If a plant has mildew, insect damage, or other problems, either throw it in the trash, burn it, or put it with other diseased plant refuse on a special pile away from the rest of the garden.

Then mulch your perennials to protect them from winter's extremes. Leaves chopped by a mower are excellent, though they tend to blow away. Straw is fine, but it can carry seeds that sprout among the flowers. Sawdust is good but can be difficult to rake away completely in the spring. Grass clippings should be avoided as a winter mulch because they tend to clump and smother the plants.

In the spring, usually in mid-March, check under the mulch to see if the perennials or any bulbs are sending out new growth. If they are, gently rake away the mulch and add it to the compost heap.

Fertilize your perennials in April or May with a slow-release fertilizer, but be careful not to overdo it. Too much nitrogen will result in tall, leafy plants with few flowers. A nonchemical fertilizer alternative is to spread about one-half inch of compost over the perennial bed in late March after any winter mulch has been removed.

Don't be afraid to move your perennials around. Think of them as being a little like the furniture in your living room. You just keep arranging and rearranging until it all looks right. If a perennial is too high for the front of a border or clashes with the plant next to it, dig it up in the early spring and move it to a different spot. However, try not to move plants more than every other year or so, or you'll prevent them from reaching peak maturity and maximum flowering.

After three or four years, many perennials get too large. They develop into large clumps with a dead spot in the middle, or their flower production is greatly reduced. That means it's time to dig them up and divide them with a spade or spading fork, gently breaking the plant into five or six new plants. Work some compost into the old hole to improve the soil, and replant one of the plants. The others can be given away or planted elsewhere in your garden. Water the new plant well.

For a listing of the best perennials to plant in an Iowa garden, see pages 124–129.

Herbs

Herbs have been valued since almost the beginning of humanity. For thousands of years, they have been treasured for medicines and flavoring food, as well as for their scent and beauty. It's no wonder that millions of gardeners often make herbs the first plants in their gardens.

Herbs can be grown from seed, but perennial herbs in particular can take a while (two to three years) to get to full size. If you want just a few common herbs, you can buy established plants at a greenhouse. If you want unusual herbs, you can order them from a specialty catalog (see pages 136–139) or you may have to grow them from seed.

There is no need to have a special herb garden. Many plants that are considered ornamental plants—digitalis, bee balm, yarrow, roses, violets—are also considered herbs by many. Herbs look good and function well planted among annuals and perennials or on the edge of the vegetable garden.

Still, it's fun to have a spot just for herbs. A small but pretty herb garden can be created on a sunny patch of lawn by creating four four-by-four-foot raised beds with eight-inch-wide pressure-treated boards. Arrange them in a square with paths three feet wide between. In the center, place a focal point, such as a bird bath, sundial, or statue. Plant with your favorite herbs.

Most people grow herbs such as basil, oregano, thyme, rosemary, and parsley for cooking. They're best fresh, and their quality is at its peak before they set flowers. To harvest them, pick them early in the day once the dew has dried off them. Store them in the refrigerator by wrapping them loosely in damp paper towels and putting them in an unfastened plastic bag. If you have a large bunch of herbs, such as basil, you can simply put their cut ends into a jar of water the way you would flowers and keep them in the refrigerator for a week or more.

To dry herbs, harvest them as specified previously. Wrap their stems with twine or cotton string, and hang them upside down in a cool, dry, well-ventilated place out of direct sunlight, such as a garage, pantry, or laundry room.

In the fall you can dig up both annual and perennial herbs, put them in pots, and keep them over the winter in a very sunny window, usually a south-facing window, or under a grow light. In the spring, plant them outdoors once again.

TIP

To contain plants that spread quickly and can become invasive (such as mint and lily-of-the-valley), plant them in a piece of sewer pipe or a bucket or plastic pot with the bottom cut or knocked out.
LUCILLE KEELING,
FEDERATED
FLOWER ART CLUB,
CEDAR FALLS

FAVORITE HERBS AND THEIR USES

Basil. An annual. Many varieties are available, but for general cooking stick to the plain green varieties. A basic ingredient of pesto and a classic with almost any tomato dish.

Chives. A perennial. Good for salads and snipping onto baked potatoes and egg and cheese dishes. Grows easily from seed.

Coriander or cilantro. An annual. Its distinctive flavor makes it a must for many Mexican and Asian dishes.

French tarragon. A perennial. French tarragon has far better flavor than the Russian tarragon often sold. Excellent with chicken, fish, or eggs. Good for making a tarragon vinegar for salads. Also good to snip into salads.

Lavender. A perennial in warmer parts of the country but often dies out during Iowa's colder winters. Doesn't like poor drainage or too much water. Highly fragrant flowers dry well and make excellent potpourris.

Marjoram. A perennial. Excellent in meat dishes, salads, fish dishes, and creamy soups.

Mint. A perennial. Plant in a bucket or large pot with the bottom knocked out so the plant won't become invasive. Excellent snipped over fruit salads. A handful of leaves steeped in a quart of boiling water make a refreshing hot or cold tea.

Oregano. A perennial. Good in nearly any dish but particularly well known in Italian cooking. Excellent in tomato-based dishes.

Parsley. A biennial that should be treated as an annual. The curly-leaved type is popular, but the flat-leaved Italian varieties are prized for their flavor. Use as a garnish, or snip into salads, stews, and just about anything else to give them a "green" flavor.

Rosemary. An annual. Excellent with chicken or lamb. In the spring, plant in a large pot sunk into the soil. In the fall, bring indoors and place in a sunny southern window. Plant outdoors again in spring.

Sage. A perennial in warmer parts of the country but sometimes dies out during Iowa's colder winters. A classic fall seasoning for chicken, stuffing, and pork.

Thyme. A perennial. Good with poultry, fish, and pork and in soups. Many types available, including lemon and those with variegated leaves.

MAY CHECKLIST

🌿 Plant corn, squash, cucumber, and melon seeds when the soil has warmed to at least sixty-five degrees. (You can measure soil temperature with a soil thermometer.) This is usually in late May. To have nearly two months of sweet corn harvests, plant early, mid-season, and late-season varieties. Also, make two plantings of each variety two weeks apart to further assure a slow, steady supply of sweet corn.

🌿 Except for the preceding seeds, just about everything can be planted outdoors after May 10 in the southern half of the state and May 15 in the northern half. After that, there is nearly no danger of frost.

🌿 Plant gladiolus corms, canna rhizomes, and tuberous begonia tubers.

🌿 "Harden off," that is, acclimate, newly purchased seedlings before you plant them outdoors. A week before planting, leave them outdoors for a couple of hours the first day. Gradually increase the time they're exposed to the sun, wind, and cool temperatures. Leave them out a couple of nights as long as temperatures aren't predicted to drop into the thirties.

🌿 Don't bother to use those undersized round wire supports for most tomato plants. They're only a few feet high, and many tomatoes grow six feet or taller. Instead, install eight-foot-long rot-resistant stakes (you can get these at a lumberyard). Bury the stakes one foot deep so that they're seven feet high. As the tomato plants grow, tie them to the stake with soft rags or strips of panty hose. Or create vertical tunnels of hog wire about six feet high, and stand them on one end around the tomatoes to support them. Stake for protection from winds. Install these and all plant supports now while the plants are still young.

Remove flowers on any strawberries you planted this year. It diverts their energy into root development critical for good production later on.

Don't remove or trim foliage of daffodils, tulips, or other bulbs until it has turned completely brown and pulls off with no resistance. The bulbs need the dying foliage to rejuvenate them for next year. If tulips have been in the ground two or three years and are leggy or blooming poorly, dig them up and discard. Tulips usually last only a few years.

Using wooden or metal markers, mark the bare spots in your garden where you need color from spring-blooming bulbs and should plant with bulbs in the fall. Specify what type of bulb and what color are needed on the marker. This helps you figure out exactly how many bulbs you need to plant in the fall and prevents your digging up old bulbs while planting new bulbs.

Mow your lawn to a height of about two inches. The clippings make excellent mulch for flower and vegetable gardens, as long as you haven't treated your yard with a herbicide. Keep the lawn well mowed throughout the season—it's one of the best ways to prevent weeds.

If you've kept Easter lily plants, plant them about four inches deep in a sunny location in your garden. They should bloom again in July. Mulch in the fall, but Easter lilies often die out during Iowa's harsh winters.

Prune suckers off those plants prone to suckering, including crabapples and other fruit trees, white poplar, chokecherry, lilacs, and American linden. You can also dig up the sucker to create a new plant. However, suckers dug up from grafted plants (which include most fruit trees) will not be identical to the parent plant.

❧ Feed roses. You can use a general outdoor plant fertilizer or one made specifically for roses. Feed about once a month until August.

❧ Keep flowers "deadheaded," that is, the spent blooms pinched or cut off. This not only keeps your garden looking tidy, it encourages better flower production.

❧ Sow grass seed now. Keep well and evenly watered.

❧ Fertilize potted plants once a month. Their requirement of constant watering results in many nutrients being flushed from the soil.

❧ Pinch mums until the Fourth of July. This will encourage bushier plants with more flowers.

❧ Keep newly planted trees and shrubs well watered.

❧ Very early in the month, take control of self-sown plants. Flowers such as larkspur, ox-eye daisies, coreopsis, hollyhocks, garden phlox, columbine, and foxglove love to reseed themselves. If you want, just let them grow where they may. But for bigger impact and a more controlled look, carefully dig up the scattered seedlings, group them together in the same spot, and water well. Ruthlessly discard or give away the seedlings you don't want.

WILDFLOWERS FOR IOWA

If you want to find out which flowers do best in Iowa, look no further than the ditch.

There, among the trash and rubble, you might find flowers that were in Iowa long before the white settlers. They've survived droughts, floods, heat, and cold. They're not fussy about soil and resist disease. Who couldn't love plants like that?

When planting wildflowers, determine how much of a purist you want to be. Truly wild plants tend to be scraggly and invasive and have small blooms that don't last more than a week or two. On the other hand, they tend to be tougher, spread themselves readily, and look fine in a semiwild setting.

Hybrid varieties of these wildflowers usually have a neater growth habit than the original, don't take over a garden, and have larger, prettier blooms that last longer. They can look out of place, however, in a wild meadow or naturalistic woodland and are more likely to succumb to adverse conditions.

Also decide how you want to define a wildflower. Not all wildflowers are native plants. Daylilies have naturalized themselves all over the state, escapees from gardens a hundred years ago. They're not native to Iowa, but they survive well on their own, and some classify them as wildflowers.

Other plants are truly wildflowers, but not necessarily in Iowa. They may have originated in Wisconsin or Ohio or even California but thrive in Iowa, too.

Hybridized wildflowers tend to do well in backyard gardens in beds and borders, where their tamer habits serve gardeners well. They are fairly noninvasive and tend to be drought resistant when planted in the right spot. True wildflowers tend to do better in large, undefined spaces, such as the corner of a field, a wooded lot, or a ditch.

You can incorporate wildflowers into your garden in several ways. You can buy established plants at a nursery and transplant them in your garden. You can buy seed of individual wildflowers and start them yourself indoors or directly in the garden. (Both methods are excellent for traditional gardens, where neatness is at a premium.) Or you can buy one of the wildflower "carpets" now available—which generally do work, though the effect is too much like a bed of weeds for some tastes. Or, if you want a large-scale planting, the packets of wildflower mix are ideal.

Some gardeners buy a can of wildflower seed mix, walk into a field, and scatter the seed, thinking it will take root. But planting a wildflower meadow is much like planting a lawn. You usually need a very sunny

WILDFLOWERS FOR SUN

Bachelor's-button
Bee balm
Black-eyed Susan
Blanketflower
California poppies
Compass plant
Coreopsis (or tickseed)
Cosmos
False-indigo
Goldenrod
Liatris (or Kansas gayfeather)
Lythrum (or loosestrife—be certain that it is a hybrid that won't become invasive; wild lythrum is classified as a noxious weed in Iowa.)
Missouri primrose
New England aster
Ox-eye daisy
Pasqueflower
Phlox
Prairie-dock
Purple coneflower
Queen Anne's lace
Rattlesnake-master
Sunflowers
Thistle
Toadflax

Bloodroot
Cardinal flower
Columbine
Dog-tooth violet
Dutchman's-breeches
Foamflower
Jack-in-the-pulpit
Jacob's ladder
Mayapple
Shooting-star
Solomon's-seal
Spiderwort
Trillium
Wild ginger

site and must first till the soil to rid it of any competing grass or weeds. You should wait a week or two for the annual weeds to germinate and then till again. Plant the wildflower seed, and work it very lightly into the soil to discourage birds from eating it. Keep evenly moist. As the flowers establish themselves, pull any large weeds. The following year you may want to reseed with annual flowers—they're the ones that provide the longest periods of bright color. In following years, you may want to replant sections of your meadow if weeds or other unwanted plants start taking over.

Don't get discouraged the first year. It may take two or more years before a wildflower meadow looks like anything more than a weed patch.

Mow the meadow each fall, and leave the cuttings to encourage plants to reseed themselves.

Wildflowers are also an excellent choice for those shady corners of the yard under trees that you don't know what to do with. Create a wood-chip or stone path that winds through the area, and surround it with woodland flowers.

No matter where you plant your wildflowers, you'll find they contribute wonderfully to a casual garden that demands little.

Roses for Iowa

Roses undeservedly have a reputation for fussiness. True, many of the hybrid teas demand pampering during the summer and heavy protection during the winter (and even then still can die out), but choose your rose carefully from the many other beautiful types available, and you can have an easy-care rose garden that's the envy of any southerner.

The key is to look for roses that are very, very hardy. Don't limit yourself to garden centers, which for practicality's sake often limit themselves to what sells best. Also leaf through several catalogs specializing in roses (see pages 136–139). No matter where you purchase your roses, skepticism is your best defense against dead roses. Even if you live in USDA Zone 5, which is southern Iowa, ignore roses with descriptions that claim a rose is hardy to Zone 5. Instead, choose a rose that is hardy to Zone 4 or better yet, Zone 3. As a rule of thumb, buy only those roses that are at least one USDA zone hardier than your own. To be absolutely safe, buy roses that are two USDA zones hardier.

Don't believe all those breathless ads about the new "carefree" roses that are supposed to make excellent hedges. They are indeed easier to care for and tougher than many other roses, but some Iowa gardeners have spent hundreds of dollars on these plants only to find out that each winter, a few more die out.

Instead, look to the supertough rugosa roses, civilized cousins of the wild rose. (If you want to plant our state flower, the wild rose, in your backyard, choose *Rosa rugosa* "Arizona.") Rugosa roses not only are cold resistant, they're also more disease resistant than some of their fussier relatives. Excellent rugosa roses include "Roseraie de l'Hay," a shrub that grows up to seven feet tall with wine red blossoms and deep fragrance; "Therese Bugnet," which grows about five feet high and has pink flowers and a deep fragrance; "Sir Thomas Lipton," which has white, fragrant flowers and grows about four feet high; and "Linda Campbell," which is one of the best of the reds. But don't expect rugosa roses to look like the classic, hybrid tea roses. They're smaller and resemble a wilder version of a cabbage rose.

For more classic-looking roses that are also very hardy, consider Griffith Buck roses, bred by the late Dr. Griffith J. Buck, a horticulture professor at Iowa State University. Griffith Buck varieties include "Applejack," "Carefree Beauty," "Country Dancer," "Hawkeye Belle," and "Prairie Princess."

Many of the floribundas and other shrub roses also

When removing flowers from your lilac bushes, don't cut too far down the stem. The tiny buds near the terminal leaf are the beginning of next year's bloom.

LEONA ONKEN,
MONTICELLO
GARDEN CLUB

do well in Iowa. The key is checking their hardiness.

Simply because a rose that you have your heart set on is listed as hardy only as far north as your USDA zone, it doesn't mean that it's doomed. Many of these roses will thrive for years—but their chances of dying out are far greater than those of hardier varieties.

While poring over the rose catalogs, trying to decide on the right rose for your garden, prepare to be a little confused. There are seemingly dozens of categories of roses, and even rose experts themselves clump different roses in different categories. It's fun to learn about roses, but you don't have to get too wrapped up in distinguishing a damask from an alba.

After you've selected a rose, prepare the soil in which to plant it. Dig a hole two to three times the size of the pot or root ball. Work plenty of compost into the hole, about three or four gallons of compost into a single planting hole. To promote drainage, which is critical for roses, many gardeners like to put several inches of river gravel, broken flower pots, broken bricks, or other such materials in the bottom of the planting hole. Then follow the planting instructions included with your rose.

Roses are heavy feeders, so fertilize them three times during the summer, once a month in May, June, and July. Don't fertilize after that. It only promotes tender new growth that's likely to be killed during the winter. To prepare roses for winter, some gardeners prune their roses in early November. However, one school of thought is that pruning back roses reduces the plant's chance of surviving the winter. Also, if you want a large rose bush, cutting it back severely each winter will make such size hard to achieve.

Either way, in early November, mound soil or compost around the base of the rose to protect its lower parts. Mound the soil about a foot high, if possible (far less, of course, on miniature roses). Most climbers should be taken down from their trellises, laid on the ground, and covered completely with soil.

All but the hardiest roses also need further protection with burlap in late November or early December. There are several methods to protect with burlap. One is to wrap the rose in burlap and tie it tightly with twine. Another is to create a miniature fence around the bush by putting several stakes in the ground in a circle around the plant. Staple burlaplike fencing around it. Fill with chopped autumn leaves. (White cones have been a popular way to protect roses but are no longer recommended because of questions about their effectiveness.)

In early April, remove burlap from roses. Remove the soil from climbers. In late April, hose off or gently scrape off the mounded soil from rose bushes.

New growth should be apparent. Prune out any dead wood. Also prune to make sure there aren't any crowded or rubbing branches. Cut the stem at a forty-five-degree angle sloping toward the center of the bush. Cut just above a bud that's facing away from the center of the shrub.

Starting in May, fertilize monthly until August. Keep faded roses trimmed off to promote continual blooming.

In Iowa, some of roses' biggest disease problems are black spot, powdery mildew, and aphids. The symptoms of black spot, as the name implies, are black spots on the foliage. Powdery mildew occurs as a grayish, often fuzzy growth on leaves. Both black spot and powdery mildew are fungal diseases that are controlled in similar ways. To prevent either, throw away fallen or dead leaves from your roses. Avoid wetting the leaves when watering. And when either disease hits, consider using a fungicide for more severe cases.

Aphids are tiny insects that suck on roses and sometimes leave behind a sticky substance. Aphids can be controlled by spraying the rose with a strong stream of water. For more severe infestations, try spraying with soapy water or a commercial insecticide.

ROSE TYPES

Climbing roses: Just about any roses with tall canes. Some David Austin roses, for example, can be used as climbers when pruned properly. However, most climbers aren't hardy in Iowa without substantial protection. To protect climbing roses, in the fall you must pull the canes off their supports, stake them to the ground, and cover completely with soil. In late April, uncover them and tie back on the supports. A simpler way to get the same effect is to use the superhardy rugosa roses pruned to grow narrow and tall. Or plant one of the few extremely cold-hardy climbers, which need only a few shovelfuls of compost around the base for winter protection. These include "Henry Kelsey," "William Baffin," "Santana," "John Davis," "Rosanna," "Salita," "Leverkusen," "Casablanca," and "Isle Krohn Superior." All are available through The Roseraie at Bayfields (see page 138).

David Austin or English roses. A relatively new development in the rose world. Have the lovely old-fashioned forms of Old Garden roses along with their beautiful scents. But unlike Old Garden roses, these roses tend to bloom continuously. Choose carefully since they tend to be marginally hardy in Iowa.

Floribunda roses. Produce an abundance of flowers, hence their name. Tend to be tall and have long stems excellent for cutting. A good landscape rose because of their bushiness and long-bloom periods. Good disease resistance. Excellent in larger flower borders. Hardiness varies.

Grandiflora roses. Classic cup shape and long stems make these wonderful for cutting. Also a bushy shape, fairly hardy, and continual flowering. Tend to be very tall plants. Good for the back of a flower border. Hardiness varies.

Griffith Buck roses. Iowa State University rose breeder Griffith Buck worked hard to breed roses that would thrive in Iowa's cold climate yet have a variety of flower forms, colors, and fragrances. Very hardy.

Hybrid tea roses. Valued for their classic rose shape and excellence as a cut flower. Tend to bloom often. Neat growing habit but have long stalks that can be unsightly. Ideal for a cutting garden. Hardiness varies, but many varieties are not reliable in Iowa.

Meidiland roses. Fairly hardy and low-maintenance roses developed in France by the House of Meidiland. Some need no pruning, only a light shearing with hedge clippers. While some are hardy to Zone 4, some are hardy only as far north as Zone 5.

Miniature roses. Tiny rose bushes that usually grow less than two feet tall with diminutive flowers. Pretty when grown as annuals in containers. Suitable for Iowa because their small size makes them easier to protect.

Old garden, heirloom, or antique roses. Any roses that predate the introduction of the hybrid tea rose in 1867. Lovely forms, easy care, good fragrance. Include cabbage roses (also known as centifolias), china roses, damasks, hybrid perpetual bloomers, gallacias, bourbons, and noisettes. Hardiness varies, but many, such as the gallacias, are fairly hardy.

Polyantha roses. Low-growing plants covered with clusters of small flowers. Hardiness varies.

Rugosa and species roses. The original roses. Very hardy, some even to Zone 2. These roses are unlike others in that they can die back to the ground and come back the next year. Very disease resistant. A variety of flower forms.

Tree roses. Roses that have been trained so that they have a long "trunk" a few feet high, topped with leaves and flowers. Very tender. Best grown in Iowa in containers that can be brought indoors for the winter.

LAWN CARE BASICS

Just as a carefully selected frame sets off a beautiful painting, so too does a well-cared-for lawn set off a beautiful garden.

Too many people think that a lawn is all there is to a garden. That's not true, any more than the frame alone makes a work of art. But a good lawn can set off flowers, shrubs, and trees in a way almost nothing else can.

Lawn-care fanatics will tell you that an attractive lawn can be achieved only through brutally hard work. They're the ones out there loaded down with sprayer and hose, hunting the lone rogue weed to blast with a shot of chemicals. They rev up huge riding mowers three times a week and water so meticulously they measure rainfall in one-hundredths of an inch.

All that's not necessary. A lawn takes attention, but if you make it a priority to keep it mowed at a proper height, an established lawn will almost take care of itself.

Mowing correctly (not too short, please) conserves water and prevents weeds, the two biggest lawn-care headaches. In the spring, keep the grass at a height of about two and a half inches. As the weather becomes hot, around late June or early July, mow to three inches.

Lawn chemicals are a source of confusion and debate. You can go a year or two without lawn chemicals and have an adequate lawn, but if you want it to be green and lush, you'll have to find some way to feed it.

If you opt for chemicals, go for two chemical applications: first, an application of a combination fertilizer and pre-emergent weed killer in April and then an application of a combination fertilizer and broadleaf weed killer in September or early October.

If you want to take a minimalist, organic approach to lawn care, simply feed your lawn once in September or early October with an organic lawn fertilizer. Application rates can vary, but the rule of thumb is one pound nitrogen per one thousand square feet.

Iowa State University has developed an organic weed killer, one of the few on the market. Made from corn, it's available mail-order through Gardens Alive! (see page 137 for ordering information).

If you aren't opposed to chemicals, you can apply a broadleaf herbicide in the fall once every two or three years. Then you can also apply a pre-emergent herbicide in the spring once every two or three years. This will keep the worst of the weeds, such as crabgrass and dandelions, in check.

Watering a lawn is simple, as long as you have a rain gauge. The rule of thumb is that lawns (and most of your garden, for that matter) need one inch of rain a week. If you receive a quarter inch of rain in one week, apply three-quarters of an inch of water. You can measure how much water you've applied to your lawn by putting a cake pan or other wide container in the area being watered. When an inch of water accumulates in the container, you know you've applied one inch to the lawn as well.

If you don't mind brownish grass, you can let your lawn go dormant in the hot, dry months of late July and August without any long-term ill effects. The only thing to be careful of is not bringing the lawn in and out of dormancy. If you are going to withhold water during those months, do it.

Don't give your lawn occasional light waterings. Instead, follow the one-inch-a-week rule and water once a week, all at once. Or, if you prefer, water it one-half inch at a time twice a week.

Water early in the morning to conserve water. During a hot afternoon, as much as half the water coming out of your sprinkler can evaporate before it hits the ground. And early morning watering gives the water plenty of time to evaporate off the leaf blades, preventing lawn diseases that thrive in damp conditions.

An easy way to make watering less of a hassle is to purchase a timer for your garden hose. It can be set to go off and on even when you're asleep or away from home.

Pets can be a problem for lawns. Dogs that urinate on lawns kill the grass in those spots. One solution, which requires much diligence, is to douse the area with a bucket of water immediately after the dog urinates. An easier solution is to train the dog to urinate on a single designated spot that has been mulched or covered with gravel.

Gardeners with shady yards often have a difficult time keeping lawns healthy. Tree roots compete for moisture and make mowing difficult. It helps to select carefully grasses that thrive in light shade, such as creeping red fescue, Chewing, or hard fescue. And it's also helpful to make sure all leaves are immediately raked to allow the maximum amount of sun reaching the grass. Lower branches of trees can be pruned off the bottom ten, twenty, or even thirty feet of mature trees to allow more light onto the ground beneath them.

But as with all garden problems, the best solution usually is working with nature rather than against it. If the problem is under just one or two trees, consider creating a bed underneath the tree. Plant it with shade-loving flowers, ferns, or ground cover. These

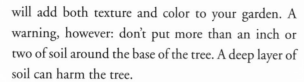
Planting marigolds among your bush beans will discourage bean beetles.

KATHRYN SCHILLING,
TIPTON GARDEN CLUB

will add both texture and color to your garden. A warning, however: don't put more than an inch or two of soil around the base of the tree. A deep layer of soil can harm the tree.

If you have a yard that is nearly all shade because of a number of mature trees, consider making it a wood-land garden with paths of shredded wood chips or flagstones weaving through it. The rest can be planted with mosses (especially if the soil is acidic and moss is growing anyway), ferns, shade-loving blooming perennials and annuals, shrubs, bulbs, ground covers, and other plants. The effect can be enchanting.

PLANTS IN CONTAINERS

Containers are a gardener's great problem solvers.

Don't have much space? Create a patio garden in containers. Too much shade? Rotate plants in containers between shady and sunny places, and you can have sun-loving plants anywhere. Like flowers but don't like the hassle? Containers are fairly low maintenance.

Just about anything in the world can be a container, as long as it has drainage holes in the bottom. (You can make holes in the bottoms of plastic containers by heating a nail over a candle flame and using the hot metal to punch holes.)

A huge variety of attractive pots are now available. Many are terra-cotta, but beware of the largest (and most expensive). Leaving a clay pot out during Iowa's harsh winter will make it shatter. If you want to use these pots, you must haul them into a garage or other sheltered place for winter storage. Or take the time to seek out the few really good terra-cotta look-alikes now available, made from fiberglass.

Pots made out of bonded stone are beautiful but are hard to find. Concrete containers are an option, but they're less attractive. You can mellow the harsh look of concrete by keeping the exterior of the pot as damp and shaded as possible; it encourages the growth of moss. If you look around, you can also find concrete containers that are colored and fairly attractive.

Other containers include decorative tins, teapots (if you can drill a hole), wicker or wire baskets (line with sphagnum moss first to hold the soil), watering cans, and just about anything else. You can even plant in an old wooden wagon.

A simple planter can be made by nailing together five pieces of rot-resistant lumber. Drill holes in the bottom for drainage. You can paint it or, especially if it's redwood or cedar, leave it plain and let it weather.

Window boxes are charming containers, and it's easy to make a simple box yourself. There are a number of window boxes available already made, but a window box should be as wide as the window. Buy the right size, if you can find it. Otherwise, build it yourself. If your woodworking skills are limited, you'll have to rely on a carpenter or skilled friend.

The one drawback of container gardens is their need for water. In the hottest days of July and August, container gardens need watering daily. If they're in a sunbaked area, they might even need watering twice a day.

Reduce the need for watering by filling pots with

top-quality soil. If the pot is very large, say twenty-four inches high, save money by filling the bottom half with ordinary garden soil mixed with perlite. Then fill the top twelve inches with the more costly good-quality potting soil.

Technology also can come to the rescue. A special sort of crystal, available at garden centers, has been developed, which greatly increases the water-holding capacity of soil. Hard water crystals that you soak in water and watch expand into clear globules are worked into the soil. They retain water and reduce the amount and frequency of watering.

Container plantings need more frequent fertilization than do plantings in the ground. All that watering flushes many of the nutrients from the soil. Fertilize lightly about once a month, or work a slow-release fertilizer into the soil at planting time.

Too often, only annuals are planted in containers. But a number of perennials are ideally suited to con-

tainer culture, including miniature roses, a number of bulbs that aren't winter hardy, herbs, cacti, dwarf fruit trees and evergreens, strawberries, and ornamental grasses. These perennials must be brought into a place that doesn't get below freezing in winter, such as a heated garage.

You can maximize your container plantings with wire trellises. Shaped as globes, pyramids, animals, and just about everything else, these forms stick into the pot for a sort of casual topiary. They're available through specialty garden suppliers, or you can make your own from wire. Train ivy, morning glories, scarlet runner bean, black-eyed Susan vine, and other vines to grow up them. Your container gardens will be every bit as attractive as the garden you create with far more space.

SHADE GARDENING

Shade is lovely, cool, and inviting for people. It's entirely different for some of our most popular garden plants.

Many yards, especially around older homes, have beautiful mature shade trees. The trees are so beautiful, in fact, that their owners are rightly reluctant to cut them down simply to get some sunlight to grow sun-loving plants.

Gardening in the shade is difficult, not because shade-loving plants are hard to grow but because we've been trained to think of gardens and yards as bright expanses of green lawn with a couple of trees and some intensely bright flower beds. And we're just not well acquainted with shade-loving plants. Everyone knows what a rose or an iris looks like, but what about the dramatically beautiful snakeroot? (It also doesn't help that some of the prettiest shade plants have some of the most awful names—lungwort, goat's-beard, and so on.)

Many gardeners think they can't garden seriously because they have so much shade. But they're selling their yards short. Shade gardens are subtle, complex, and therefore beautiful.

If you feel you must have more sun, there are a few options. One is to eliminate the trees and shrubs that are creating the shade. However, if you're like most gardeners, you love the very obstacles that are blocking the light. And removing forty-foot trees is no simple business.

You can, however, trim lower branches. This raises and thins the canopy of a tree and allows in more light. It's an especially good option for pines or other evergreens whose lower branches are browning and droopy.

Evaluate your shrubs as well. Too many people are attached to overgrown junipers, lilacs, or yews that are in truly dreadful shape and threaten to overwhelm a whole side of their house. You may have to get tough and bring out the chain saw and remove them completely. You can then replant more modest-sized shrubs at a proper distance from each other and your house.

Then evaluate how much light you're left with. In deepest shade, you'll be limited to ferns, mosses, and a few other tough plants. Light shade can support a number of plants, including many blooming plants prized for their shots of color.

An area with light, dappled, or open shade gets no more than three or four hours of shade a day. It's often under a high canopy of trees. There's usually quite a

bit of sun, and a wide variety of plants can be planted in this area. Many roses usually do well in this type of light, as do a number of perennials that like a little shade. Strawberries and lettuces, for example, tolerate very light shade.

A partially shady area gets shade four to six hours a day. It might get shade in the afternoon or just in the morning. The shade is often caused by the shadow of a house or building, the immediate north side of a building being a perfect example. Shade-loving rhododendrons and azaleas, astilbe, begonias, digitalis, trollius, and many other plants do very well in partial shade.

A medium shady area is usually open, such as the spot underneath a mature shade tree near a house, but it gets no direct sunlight. It might have lots of indirect light because, for example, it's next to a paved area, which reflects light. Hostas, daylilies, coleus, and impatiens do well in these conditions.

An area with heavy shade gets very little light. It's usually underneath shrubs or several trees planted close together or between fences or buildings. Only ferns, mosses, some hostas, and a few other plants thrive in these conditions.

There's no science to figuring out what type of shade you have and what will do well in a particular spot. The best way to determine the type of shade is simply to plant something there and see how it does. If it doesn't do well, move it someplace else, a method that's been dubbed "trowel and error." Get yourself on the mailing list of at least one of the several catalogs that specialize in shade gardening (see pages 136–139) and start experimenting to see what works in your particular conditions.

Shade gardening under some trees, such as maples, can be problematic because their shallow roots compete with other plants for moisture. You cannot simply build up the soil over the roots because that can kill the tree. In such a case, seek out plants that thrive in dry shade, such as *Vinca minor*, perennial violets, some hardy geraniums, foxglove, and columbine.

If your shady spot is covered with moss, consider encouraging the moss rather than killing it. The Irish and Japanese, for example, have entire gardens of moss. Some rocky slopes in Iowa's state parks have a stunning array of mosses, making a lush green tapestry of what would otherwise be merely a rocky slope. Encourage moss on partially buried boulders, statues, pots, or stone or concrete benches by pulling up bits of it and placing it on damp stone.

Several shrubs, including hydrangeas and rhododendrons, both of which have beautiful flowers, thrive in acidic soil and shade. In Iowa, however, make sure you choose from among only a handful of varieties, such as the PJM rhododendrons or the Peegee hydrangeas, that will survive our harsh winters.

Many early spring-blooming bulbs—such as crocus, daffodils, scilla, and grape hyacinths—thrive under trees that drop their leaves over the winter. Until the trees begin to leaf out, plants receive plenty of light and provide lots of color.

One of the best things you can do for your shade garden is to stop worrying about having lots of color. A peaceful green oasis can be one of the loveliest gardens around. One Ames restaurant built an entire wall of large windows next to a grove of trees that are underplanted with nothing but cinnamon ferns. On a hot summer evening, there's not a more cooling, restful view in town.

PLANTS THAT THRIVE IN SHADE

BULBS	PERENNIALS	SHRUBS
Caladium* (p to m)	Astilbe (l to p)	Barberry (l to p)—make sure variety
Daffodils** (l)	Bergenia (l to p)	is hardy in Iowa
Dwarf daffodils** (l)	Bleeding-heart (l to p)	Hydrangea (l to f)
Dwarf iris** (l)	Campanula (l)	Rhododendron and azalea (l)
Lilies, some varieties (l)	Cardinal flower (l to p)	Viburnum, some varieties (l)
Nonstop begonias* (l to m)	Columbine (l to p)	Yew (l to p)
Scilla** (l)	Coralbells (l to p)	
Snowdrops** (l)	Cranesbill or hardy geranium (l)	
Windflowers** (l)	Daylilies (l to p)	**GROUND COVERS**
Wood hyacinths** (l)	Digitalis or foxglove (l to p)	
	Goat's-beard (l to p)	Ajuga (l to p)
	Jabob's-ladder (p)	Lily-of-the-valley (l to m)
ANNUALS	Lady's-mantle (l to p)	Pachysandra (p to m)
	Ligularia (p)	Sweet woodruff (p)
Browallia (l)	Liriope (l to p)	Vinca minor (l to f)
Coleus (l to p)	Loosestrife (l)	Wild ginger (l to m)
Impatiens (l to p)	Lungwort (p)	
New Guinea impatiens (l to p)	Monkshood (l to p)	
Nicotiana (l)	Perennial forget-me-not (l)	l = light, dappled, or open shade
Pansies** (l)	Primulas (l to p)	p = partial shade
Violas** (l)	Snakeroot (l to p)	m = medium shade
Wax begonias (l to p)	Solomon's-seal (p to m)	f = full, heavy, or deep shade
Wishbone-flower (l to p)	Trillium (p to m)	* Not winter hardy. Must be dug up and
	Trollius (l)	stored over the winter.
	Virginia bluebells (l to m)	** Do well under deciduous trees that let in
		light in early spring and late fall.

JUNE

JUNE CHECKLIST

🌿 Plant sweet corn a second time, about two weeks after your first planting in late May, to extend the harvesting season.

🌿 Mulch to control weeds, conserve moisture, and cut down on diseases. Good mulch materials include grass clippings, chopped autumn leaves, straw, hay, and pine needles.

🌿 If cabbage worms are a problem, control them organically with *Bacillus thuringiensis*, available at some nurseries or through organic mail-order suppliers.

🌿 Stop cutting asparagus and rhubarb.

🌿 Weed your garden diligently. It's far easier to control weeds when they're small and sparse.

🌿 Pinch chrysanthemum buds. Keep pinching until July for fuller, bushier plants.

🌿 Start broccoli plants from seed indoors to plant in the garden in mid-July.

🌿 Check out clearance sales on garden supplies and plants. Buy only healthy-looking plants. There are more sales to be had in the bulb catalogs. Many offer 10 percent or more off if you order early.

🌿 Keep flowers "deadheaded," that is, the spent blossoms pinched or cut off, to encourage continual bloom.

🌿 Don't harvest or handle green beans when the plants are wet. Doing so will transmit disease.

🌿 Lettuce will start to bolt (send up a long seed stalk) this month. When it bolts, the leaves become bitter, so pull plants out and discard.

🌿 Get rid of weeds growing in the cracks of pavement by spraying them with a herbicide, or use undiluted chlorine bleach, a less expensive and more earth-friendly substitute.

🌿 If you want to use chemicals on your tomatoes, begin weekly applications of a fungicide to control disease.

🌿 Keep the suckers pinched off indeterminate (also known as vining) tomatoes. Suckers are the little shoots that grow at a forty-five-degree angle between the main stem and "branches" of the tomato plant. Pinching these now keeps tomatoes a manageable size and maximizes productivity.

🌿 Once you have good-sized green tomatoes, you can hasten ripening by pruning some of the plant's roots. Simply take a spade and plunge it into the soil on one side of the tomato plant, four or five inches away from the main stem.

🌿 You can continue to grow lettuce into July if you erect a shade cloth over the lettuce to cool the air and prevent bolting. Some gardeners use latticework or other methods to provide cooling shade.

🌿 Dig up and discard tulip bulbs that are more than a few years old and have been blooming poorly. Mark spots in your garden where you would like to plant bulbs in the fall with large wooden markers available at greenhouses or with other markers. Specify color and type of bulb on the marker. In the fall, you'll know how many bulbs to buy and where to plant them.

🌿 Don't water plants late in the day. Early morning watering allows moisture enough time to evaporate from plant foliage before nightfall, discouraging disease.

Fresh parsley is easy to freeze.
Just cut it, wash in cold water,
shake dry, remove the stems,
and freeze. You'll have fresh-
tasting parsley all winter.
ANN JOHNK,
AVOCA GARDEN CLUB

HEALTHY PLANTS

Sooner or later, all gardeners face them—the nasty little critters and microscopic organisms that invade gardens and ruin prized plants. As with all things, prevention is your best defense. To prevent tiny invaders, keep plants healthy in the first place. Well-watered plants planted in good soil with the right light are naturally more disease resistant. And space your plants the recommended distance from each other to make sure air flows through them, further preventing disease.

If you do spot a problem, check with your local extension agent, the Iowa State University Horticulture Answer Line (called the "Hortline"), or a nursery for the best way to remedy the problem—immediately. If you wait even a week, the disease often gets the upper hand and can kill or seriously damage your plants.

If you're hesitant to use pesticides, there are often nonchemical alternatives available. Whiteflies, for example, can be controlled by spraying plants with an insecticidal soap available at your garden center.

For more serious disease problems, especially on valuable plants such as a large shade tree, consult with the Iowa State University Plant Disease Clinic (see page 145). The service is often free.

Gather a representative sample of the disease problem and include as much of the plant as you can. Include both infected and healthy plant parts. Wrap the sample in a dry paper towel, and place it in a plastic bag. Do not seal it. Enclosing a photo of the plant is helpful. Send in a crush-proof box, or press and enclose in an envelope.

Just as you can cut down on the number of colds you have by good personal hygiene, you can cut down on the number of diseases in your garden with good horticultural hygiene. Here are some tips.

Each fall, remove dead foliage and plants from your garden. You may want to leave some plants that have winter interest, such as some sedums, remaining. But dead plant material often harbors disease.

Don't plant the same type of plant in the same place each year. That spot will become a breeding ground for the pests that plague that particular plant. Plant different plants in that spot for at least two years out of three (with the exception, of course, of perennial plants).

Don't throw diseased plants on your compost heap. You'll end up spreading disease along with your compost. Create a special spot for diseased plant material that's away from your garden, burn the diseased plant material, or throw it out in the garbage.

Plant disease-resistant plants. Many plants have been bred specifically to resist common disease. Choose these whenever possible. Older crabapple varieties, for example, are susceptible to scab. Plant the most disease-resistant varieties you can find. Disease resistance is usually described on the plant labels or in catalog descriptions.

Mulch. A thick layer of mulch not only conserves moisture in the soil, it also keeps dirt from splashing on the plants, which discourages disease.

Water in the morning. Don't water after three in the afternoon. The water will remain on the plants overnight, inviting disease.

Steer away from exotic plants. The less suited a plant is to Iowa, the more problems you'll have. There are hundreds of plants well suited to Iowa's climate, so why not stick to these instead of difficult plants—which also eat up valuable time.

TIP

Mix together one-half cup vinegar, one-half cup sugar, one or two banana peels, and one quart water. Put it in a milk jug without a lid and place in the garden. Bugs, attracted by the contents, will enter the jug and drown.
MARY SMITH,
COON RAPIDS
RURAL GARDEN CLUB

EDIBLE LANDSCAPING

Whoever said that vegetables had to go in the vegetable garden and flowers had to go in the flower bed?

Some of the most successful gardens are those that have vegetables among the flowers and vice versa. Especially when space is tight, mingling the two can make for a beautiful garden that tastes as good as it looks.

Miniature fruit trees that grow only four or five feet tall are excellent candidates for the back of the flower border. Rhubarb's large green leaves and red stalks are at home in the middle of a large flower border. And strawberries, with their lovely leaves and tiny white blossoms, are excellent edging plants. Grapes can be trained over an arbor. Asparagus sends up delicate, feathery tops that are beautiful in late summer. Red lettuces can be a striking contrast to the green foliage of a flower bed.

Many herbs also fit in well with flowers. In fact, many plants we think of as ornamental flowers also often are classified as herbs. Bee balm, for example, is valued for its pink and red flowers, but is also an herb.

Mixing flowers into the vegetable garden is more than just pretty—it's practical, too. Marigolds are supposed to prevent nematodes, for example, and nasturtiums also are believed to repel diseases.

PROPAGATING PLANTS

Gardeners can save themselves hundreds and even thousands of dollars by learning how to propagate their own plants.

Propagating is a fancy word for reproducing plants. It might sound difficult, but even beginners can give it a try. Not only does propagating your own plants save money, it's also tremendous fun.

There are several ways you can make plants in your—or a friend's—garden multiply.

Cuttings. Take a cutting from the end of a branch or stem in spring. Depending on the size of the plant, the cutting should be anywhere from three inches to eight inches long. Strip off lower leaves, and dip the end in rooting hormone, available at garden centers. Plant in a small pot filled with vermiculite for flowers and vegetables or sand for shrubs and trees. Keep moist until a root system is well established. Plant outdoors in a permanent spot, or plant in a specially prepared "nursery" bed until large enough to plant in a permanent spot.

Some plants, such as ivies and coleus, can be rooted by sticking cuttings into a glass of water. When roots are about one-half inch long, plant in soil.

Plant division. This works well with many perennial flowers. Simply dig up part of the roots with foliage still attached. The parent plant will survive, and the smaller plant can be planted in its permanent spot. Keep shaded the first day or so and well watered for at least the first week. Most ferns and hostas can be readily divided as well. Divide spring-blooming perennials, such as irises and peonies, in August or September. Divide fall- and summer-blooming perennials in late April or early May.

Collecting seeds. In the fall, many plants, especially annual vegetables and flowers, produce seeds. That's your chance to collect them for next year. To harvest seeds from flowers, wait until the flower dries up and cut it off the plant. Holding the flower over a sheet of white paper, tear the flower apart to find the seeds, and let them fall on the paper. Allow the seeds to dry several days in a small, labeled bowl. To collect from most fruits or vegetables, pick an overripe fruit or vegetable and remove the seeds. Allow the seeds to dry several days on a sheet of paper toweling. Store them in a cool, dry place, and plant in early spring.

Marigolds, cosmos, tomatoes, larkspur, snapdragons, petunias, sunflowers, peppers, melons, and squash lend themselves to seed collection. A warning, however: if the parent plant is a hybrid, its offspring might turn out quite different. Check labels and seed

packets to see if your candidate for seed collection is a hybrid.

Transplanting seedlings. Many plants freely reseed themselves or send up suckers from their roots. These tiny plants can be dug up in the spring and replanted. These include phlox, coreopsis, lilacs, crabapples, obedience plant, rudbeckia, hollyhocks, foxglove, and larkspur.

J U L Y

JULY CHECKLIST

🌾 Keep up on watering and weeding chores. Your garden will look better and have less disease. Don't allow plants to wilt.

🌾 As weather gets hot, mow the grass a little longer, about three inches high.

🌾 Check your garden daily. This will help you spot diseases and other problems immediately. Many gardeners start the day with a short stroll around the garden, coffee cup in hand.

🌾 In mid to late July, plant a second crop of vegetables for a fall harvest. Plant the seeds of radishes, beets, peas, lettuce, spinach, kale, mustard greens, turnips, rutabagas, and other vegetables that like cool weather. Keep the seeds well watered.

🌾 Fertilize roses for the last time this year late in the month. Keep faded flowers trimmed. If you see black spots on your roses, they have a disease called, logically enough, black spot. Treat it by dusting the plant with sulfur dust, available at your garden center. A grayish fuzzy substance on your roses indicates powdery mildew. Treat by spraying with a fungicide bought at your garden center. Or try an unproven but organic spray of a solution of four tablespoons baking soda and one tablespoon Murphy's Oil Soap dissolved in one gallon of water. Reapply after rain.

🌾 Suckers and water sprouts on fruit trees and shrubs (such as lilacs) need constant removal. Keep them trimmed while small.

🌾 As green beans and other vegetables begin to produce heavily, keep them harvested. Leaving mature vegetables on a plant signals it to stop production.

- Remove old raspberry canes after the plants stop producing fruit.

- Harvest onions when the tops fall over. Cure them by allowing them to dry in a cool, well-ventilated place (such as a porch) out of the rain for a week. Braid into ropes if you like. Store in net bags or the feet of old panty hose, nailed to the rafters of a dry basement, heated garage, or other cool, dark, dry place.

- You can get as many wood chips as you need free or for a small delivery fee. Contact the city or whoever collects trash in your area. They often chip brush and will deliver the chips to your house by the truckload. Use these around established shrubs and trees or in other areas without small plants. Fresh wood chips can take nitrogen from the soil, and some contain a naturally occurring growth inhibitor.

- Keep flowers "deadheaded."

- If you admire a flower in a friend's garden, be vocal about it. Other gardeners will often give you a plant slip either now or in the spring.

- If you're serious about having lettuce all summer long, despite the heat, try starting lettuce in a partly shaded spot in containers. Or transplant lettuce seedlings into the main vegetable garden with latticework or a shade cloth suspended above them.

- Order bulbs for planting next month or in early October. Ordering now assures the varieties you want. Also, ordering early sometimes gets you a discount.

Watering

During April and May, it's a delight to work the ground and pick out plants at the greenhouse. But by mid-summer, the grunge work begins: watering, watering, and more watering.

As a rule of thumb, everything in your garden needs the equivalent of one inch of water a week. Large trees, of course, don't need additional water. Neither do most shrubs that are taller than waist-high and were planted three or more years ago. Just about everything else—especially your lawn—needs a good supply of water. Depending on the year, most Iowa gardeners don't need to water their gardens regularly until June. During most weeks of March, April, and May, Iowa gets the equivalent of an inch of rain, even if it's in the form of a quarter inch here and a half inch there.

Of course, when you first plant seeds or plants, they need a thorough watering. Keep the soil moist but not soggy until the seeds have germinated or the plant becomes established, usually in a week or two.

Invest in a rain gauge. It costs just a few dollars and ensures better harvests and healthy plants. Relying on weather reports to monitor rainfall isn't very accurate. Rainfall varies by a quarter of an inch or more, even in the same town, and weather reports can't give nearly enough detail.

When it does come time to water, always water in the morning, since watering in the evening invites fungus and other diseases. Watering in the late morning and early afternoon, especially on hot days, wastes water. As much as 50 percent of the water from your sprinkler will end up not on your garden but evaporated into the air. Water in the very early morning, if possible.

When you use a sprinkler, set out a flat-bottomed dish or pan in your yard. When the pan has one inch of water in it, you know that you've applied one inch of water to your garden.

Keeping container plants watered can be tricky. In very hot weather, they may need watering daily. If they're in small pots in a very sunny spot, you might even have to water them twice a day. You can conserve water and time with container plantings by mixing in some of those gel-like crystals into your soil when you plant the plants. These crystals can be purchased at local garden centers. You add water, and the crystals swell to make a Jell-O-like clear slurry that greatly improves the soil's water retention.

To cut down on watering chores, consider buying some of the new gadgets that save time and water. An expensive but very effective way to keep your lawn watered is an underground watering system with pop-up sprinklers. It's timed to go on in the very early morning hours and can help keep a lawn perfectly watered. However, even for a small lawn, such systems can cost thousands of dollars.

For flower beds and vegetable gardens, a far less expensive option is the black-plastic soaker hoses, made from recycled tires. These hoses have thousands of tiny pores that seep water. They can be buried in the ground about one inch deep. A disadvantage of these hoses is that they make working the soil difficult. A spade in the wrong place will slice the hose neatly in two, though you can buy joiners to repair a cut hose.

Drip-emitter systems, which run tiny hoses to individual plants, can be valuable for rose gardens, thirsty shrubs, or extensive container plantings.

Whatever watering method you use, water timers can be a considerable labor saver. Water timers can be attached to the hydrant and set to water your yard for a certain number of hours. This way, you can leave the house in the morning and your timer can shut off the water, even when you're not home.

A terrific way to conserve moisture—and prevent weeds, too—is to mulch. You can use everything from gravel to grass clippings to newspapers to straw. All will prevent water from evaporating from the soil.

Use the type of mulch you think is attractive and most readily available. Lay the mulch at varying thicknesses. Straw should be laid four to six inches deep. Grass clippings should be laid three inches deep. Sawdust mulch should be about an inch deep. Wood chips should be three inches deep. Newspaper should be laid six to eight sheets thick. Other mulch materials include pine needles, chopped corncobs, and chopped or shredded autumn leaves.

To make sure your tomatoes, cucumbers, melons, and squash get enough water, sink into the ground a few inches from the plant a large tin can with the top removed and holes punched into the bottom. When watering, water the soil around the plant and also fill the can.
LEONE SAUER,
QUASQUETON
GARDEN CLUB

*To repel aphids, whiteflies,
and other garden pests, make
a repellent by combining in
a blender one garlic bulb, one
small onion, one tablespoon
cayenne pepper, and one quart
water. Let steep one hour,
then add one tablespoon
liquid soap. Spray on plants
immediately, or store in a
tightly covered container in the
refrigerator for up to one week.*

MARIE SMEDSRUD,
TOWN AND COUNTRY
GARDEN CLUB,
DECORAH

Renovating your Landscape

You've moved into a new house and the yard is a mess. There are weeds by the garage. The evergreens are horrendously overgrown. The lawn looks like chickens have scratched away everything green. What to do and where to begin?

Every yard has its special problems and its special advantages. Some of these—a precipitous slope that won't grow anything but weeds, a beautiful spreading oak out front—will be immediately apparent. Others won't unveil themselves for a few months or even a few years. What looks like an undistinguished bush in July will in April reveal itself as a gorgeous forsythia, resplendent in bright yellow blossoms. The lovely mature maples in the backyard that you loved when you saw them in September with the real estate agent end up blocking valuable light and have surface roots that make a manicured lawn impossible.

Hold back on any major landscaping until you've lived in your house for one year. By then, you'll know your landscape and its particular assets and problems.

To evaluate your landscape, step back and look at your property with a critical eye. What needs to be done? Is there hope for the evergreens if they're trimmed back? Can the lawn be renovated rather than ripped up? Make a list of priorities.

If you're completely puzzled, try tackling your yard in the following order. Or simply follow the steps that apply to your situation in the order that makes the most sense.

Cleanup. When moving into a new house, the first task is usually lawn cleanup. Don't get overly zealous and rip out every shrub in sight. Live with them for a while before you do anything drastic. But do rip out things that are obviously weeds or obviously past their prime. Rake up dead leaves. Pick up any accumulated trash. Tear out a rusting, sagging chain link fence or other dilapidated structures. Mow the lawn, even if there doesn't appear to be much of one. Prune any obviously dead wood from trees. Then sit back and take a long second look.

Decide what to do with the lawn. The biggest problem with lawns is that people want them in the most unlikely spots—on steep slopes, under shady trees, and in other difficult spots. Instead of fighting nature, work with it. If you have a steep front slope, plant it with a ground cover, a spreading shrub or evergreen, or other erosion-resistant plants that you don't have to mow. If grass won't grow under a large tree, try creating a large, abstractly shaped bed (perfect circles tend to be boring) and plant it with something that likes shade, such as hostas, bleeding-heart, daylilies, astilbe, vinca, or bishop's-weed. They can turn an ugly spot into the focal point of your yard.

If the grass is growing in a reasonably sunny, level spot but is still a mess, try to figure out why.

Is the ground bumpy and difficult to mow? Try spreading topsoil evenly and very thinly (about one-quarter inch) on the problem areas three times a year to even it out. If it's really bad, get out the spade and level it. Replant with grass seed.

Has creeping charlie or other weeds taken over? Keep the lawn mowed, and rake out and rip out by hand as much as you can. If you don't mind using pesticides, use a broadleaf herbicide in the spring or fall. Treat twice, seven days apart. If it's really bad in one small area, spray it with Roundup. This will kill everything in the area, including the grass. But in two or three months, you will be able to replant the area with grass seed.

Is the grass sparse? In the spring or fall, rake up the soil and sprinkle it heavily with a grass seed specific to the growing conditions, such as a shade mix. Rope off with stakes and twine. Keep evenly moist until the grass is established.

If the grass is sparse in a high-traffic area, consider laying some large, flat flagstones or creating a gravel or wood-chip path or play area in the problem spot.

In the fall, it's a good idea to rent a lawn aerator and remove small plugs of dirt from your lawn to alleviate soil compaction. This is hard work, however. You may want to have a lawn service do it for you.

Although many gardeners are rightly concerned about using lawn chemicals, if you have a problem lawn, you might want to consider using chemicals for one season. Once your lawn is established and healthy, you can then get by with just a spring and fall application of an organic fertilizer.

Evaluate your trees and shrubs. Many homeowners are faced with overgrown shrubs and trees. If the plant is awkward and badly formed, is blocking windows or doors, or is enveloping a house, you will have to take drastic action by either pruning it severely or removing it.

Some plants respond well to thoughtful pruning, however, so you may want to try that first and see what you're left with. Before you prune, however, do your homework. Find a book at the library or bookstore that gives specific pruning times and direction for your shrubs. Or contact your local county extension office or the Iowa State University Horticulture Answer Line for help (see page 144).

Repair or remove structures. What sort of shape is your fence in? If it threatens to topple, the wood is rotten, or the chain link is rusted, you're probably

better off ripping it out and pitching it. However, a few bad boards can be replaced. Even a rusty chain link can be spray painted an unobtrusive dark green with rust-resistant paint.

If you have a steep slope shored up with stones, concrete, or landscape timbers, you should consider having a professional repair them. Not only is repairing these yourself backbreaking work, but removing these structures incorrectly can also be dangerous. For smaller slopes, you can usually do the work yourself. A wooden deck in poor repair should be fixed or torn out.

How will you use the landscape? Do you have a place for garbage cans? Bikes? Pets? Are there paths where people walk? Do you have a convenient spot for the grill? Is a fence needed? What's the privacy like? Which views should be played up, and which should be disguised? Is there a pleasant spot to view the backyard, such as a patio or porch?

An effective way to make yourself view your landscape clearly is to take photos. On a photo, it's easy to block out an unsightly shrub with your thumb or to sketch in a different front walk with a marker.

Once you get started on renovation, keep in mind that your plans will change over the years along with your lifestyle, your energy, and your tastes. And nature might change things once or twice, too. That oak tree that's cast deep shade across the south side of your house might topple in a windstorm one day, zapping your shade plants but giving you a wealth of sun. Even with the best-laid plans, a garden is never static—and that is one of its many delights.

WILDLIFE CONTROL

Have problems with deer and other wildlife in your yard? Good luck.

There are no easy solutions to wildlife problems. Any animal that's hungry enough, desperate enough, or clever enough will outsmart the average gardener. But there are ways at least to deter the critters.

Fencing and netting nearly always work, though they're not particularly attractive and are rather expensive. Vegetable gardeners with severe all-around wildlife problems can create something of a no-critter zone in which to grow their plants. Erect a six-foot to seven-foot fence of chicken wire around the garden. The fencing should be woven tightly enough to prevent small rabbits from squeezing through. Bury the bottom of the fencing three inches into the soil to prevent rabbits from burrowing under. Stretch chicken wire across the top to keep out birds or clever raccoons. Include a gate wide enough to get a wheelbarrow through.

The toughest gardeners have hauled out a gun. Others have relied on their cats and dogs to deal with the problem. The more peaceable solution, however, is just to learn to live with the animals, maybe even appreciating the benefits of having nature up close. And console yourself with this: animal populations vary. A harsh winter can thin out deer herds. A wet spring can drown small rabbits. A wildlife problem that's terrible one year may be minimal the next.

Here are some methods for controlling wildlife that aren't proven to work but probably can't hurt.

Deer. Often called by frustrated gardeners "rats with antlers," these animals can ravage an entire yard overnight. There's not much you can do, except fence the property with deer fence. Hanging a hotel-sized bar of soap still in its wrapper from prized or young trees will deter the deer, but they often will simply go on to another plant nearby.

Woodchucks. Supposedly, these animals hate crossing black plastic, so try creating a barrier of black plastic around the plants to be protected.

Squirrels. Although squirrels can walk along wires, jump from trees, and scramble up seemingly anything, conelike squirrel baffles at least slow them down. Larger baffles are available for trees where squirrels are a problem, cracking nuts and littering the lawn. You can make your own baffles from sheet metal.

Rabbits. Fencing at least two feet high and buried three inches in the ground is your best bet, where practical. If not, some people swear by scattering hu-

🌿🌿 TIP 🌿🌿

To attract butterflies, include at least one moist spot or puddle. Butterflies like to drink from these areas and utilize the minerals there.
TRAER GARDEN CLUB

man hair or bloodmeal in their gardens. These must be replenished after each rain.

Gophers. Smoke bombs are available to drive them out of their tunnels. More expensive but supposedly more effective is a high-tech device that emits high-pitched sounds that drive them out of your yard.

Moles. These burrowing animals can create unattractive mounded tunnels in your yard. The tunnels do improve the texture of the soil, however. To get rid of moles, you can use special mole traps, but you have to place them in areas where the moles are active. Mole poison is also available.

Raccoons. These often attack corn patches. The best deterrent is fencing, especially electric fencing. Put one wire about six inches off the ground and the second about sixteen inches high. Some gardeners also recommend sprinkling hot pepper on the corn silks.

Birds. Birds that raid your berries and fruit can be deterred by draping your berries and trees with fruit netting. You can also plant a mulberry tree nearby—the birds supposedly will prefer your mulberries. However, some cities have ordinances that prohibit planting mulberries, sometimes labeled as "trash trees."

You might try hanging a pie pan in a tree to frighten off the birds. Also, in your vegetable garden it doesn't hurt to give an old-fashioned scarecrow a try. Even if it doesn't frighten off the birds, it entertains the humans.

AUGUST

AUGUST CHECKLIST

🐞 Begin new lawns now until late August in northern Iowa and until mid-September in southern Iowa.

🐞 Don't fertilize roses after the first of this month or for the remainder of the year. It would only encourage tender new growth that would be killed during the winter.

🐞 Turn compost pile every week or so to speed decomposition. Also, water occasionally to further speed decomposition.

🐞 You may want to save time and water by letting your lawn go dormant this month. Simply withhold water. The lawn will turn brown but will not die. Do not, however, bring it out of dormancy by watering it. That stresses the lawn.

🐞 Pansies, lobelia, violas, snapdragons, and other flowers that love cool weather are beginning to brown and die. Pull them up. Next year try planting flowers that bloom in hot weather, such as marigolds, petunias, and impatiens, among the others so they can fill in once the cool-loving plants die back.

🐞 Cure onions, squash, pumpkins, potatoes, and other garden vegetables before storing. Spread on newspapers in a shady, well-ventilated area protected from rain, such as a porch. Store onions and potatoes in mesh bags or old, clean panty hose in a cool, dry location. Store squash and pumpkins at room temperature.

🐞 In mid to late August, pinch off all the blossoms and new growth from your tomatoes. It will force the plants to put their energy into ripening the remaining green tomatoes before the last frost. Also, to encourage ripening in vining-type tomatoes, prune the top by several inches once they reach six feet.

- August is a good time to dig a new bed (see pages 26–27). You may have to water the area thoroughly first to loosen soil hardened by dry weather.

- Avoid pruning evergreens until late August.

- Keep "deadheading" flowers and keep weeding. And keep garden vegetables picked to encourage continued production.

- If an annual is badly damaged by disease, consider just pulling it out and discarding rather than trying to save it this late in the season. If a perennial is badly damaged, consider cutting it back to the ground.

- Pick up and destroy windfall apples and other fallen fruit to reduce the number of overwintering insects.

- Many flowers that dry well are at their prime this month. Pick them at their peak, not when they begin to fade. Tie them by the stem at their base, and hang them upside down in an airy, dark attic, closet, or garage.

- Cut back petunias if they're getting leggy. It will encourage a new flush of bloom.

SPRING-BLOOMING BULBS

Planting bulbs is an act of faith and hope. While the winter winds howl, gardeners can think happily of the bulbs tucked into the garden, ready to grow and bloom at the first hint of spring. In Iowa, bulbs are especially rewarding. After our long, difficult winters, the explosion of color provided by bulbs in an otherwise bleak, early spring landscape is cheering indeed. Tulips, daffodils, hyacinths, crocuses, scilla, grape hyacinths, and many others fill the spring garden at a time when few other plants are blooming.

Planting bulbs is simple. First select a site that gets full sun (six or more hours of direct sun a day). Early-blooming plants, such as crocuses and daffodils, can be planted under trees that lose their leaves. The leaves don't come out, shading the ground underneath them, until the bulbs have already bloomed.

Don't plant bulbs closer than three feet from the foundation of your house. The warmth generated by the house interferes with the necessary chilling of the bulbs. It also makes them send out new growth too early, only to get nipped by extreme cold.

Provide bulbs with good drainage. Planting on a gentle slope with rich, well-drained soil is ideal. Good drainage is critical with tulips. If they're in a spot where they'll be damp, the bulbs will become diseased and fail.

Plant bulbs in the last week of September or the first two or three weeks of October. The depth you plant depends on the bulbs. Use the following list as a guide, but also get specific information at the greenhouse. (Any reputable mail-order company includes detailed planting instructions.)

If you're putting the bulbs into a new bed, dig up the soil to a depth of at least eighteen inches in the area you'll be planting. Spread three inches of peat moss or compost on the soil and work it in. If there's significant clay, add plenty of sand and sprinkle with gypsum. Plant the bulbs in clumps of at least six, though clumps of ten or more are better.

If you're putting the bulbs into an existing flower bed, simply tuck them in among the flowers. Loosen the soil several inches deeper than what you'll be planting the bulb. Plant roundish bulbs with the pointed or tapered side up. Plant a few inches apart in clumps since soldier-straight rows look artificial.

Including Bulb Booster, a bulb fertilizer, in the planting hole is helpful (irises don't need this). Bonemeal is practically worthless as a bulb fertilizer because too often it's processed in a way that robs it of its nutrients.

Mulch the bulbs with chopped leaves, straw, pine needles, or another handy mulching material and water well. If the fall turns out to be dry, give them one or two more waterings before the first hard frost.

In the spring, you'll be greeted with bright flowers. After the blooms fade, leave the foliage alone. Let it die back on its own. Do not trim it off because the bulbs need it to rejuvenate for next year.

Here, in order of their bloom, are some of the most popular bulbs.

Crocuses. Blooming in late March and early April, these small bulbs (actually corms) come primarily in purple, yellow, white, and variations of these colors. They thrive in a variety of conditions. You can even plant them in your lawn or in a wooded area, a technique that is called naturalizing. They return each year and often multiply. Plant about three inches deep.

Daffodils. Blooming in early April through early May, the bright yellows, whites, and oranges of daffodils are the perfect foil for overcast early spring skies. Daffodils return each year and often multiply. Plant early, mid-season, and late varieties for the longest season of bloom. Plant about six inches deep.

Hyacinths. Blooming in late April and early May, hyacinths are intensely fragrant. They come in blue, purple, white, and pink. Usually last only two or three years. Plant about six inches deep.

Tulips. Blooming in late April and May, tulips come in a wide range of sizes, colors, and forms. Plant early, mid-season, and late varieties for the longest season of bloom. Provide excellent drainage. Usually only last two or three years before becoming too weak to bloom. Plant about seven inches deep.

Irises. Most are not technically bulbs but are planted in the fall along with spring-blooming bulbs. Come in nearly every color. German bearded irises are the most common in Iowa, but Siberian and Japanese irises also are very attractive and thrive here. Plant German bearded irises just under the surface of the soil, others as instructed on the plant label or package. German bearded irises multiply rapidly and need to be divided every four or five years.

To prevent disease in a German bearded iris, when planting, dip the rhizome (the fleshy root) in a solution of half water and half chlorine bleach for a moment. Dust with sulfur and plant.

WEEDS

It's often been said and bears repeating: a weed is just a plant in the wrong place.

Gardeners find themselves doing crazy things, like pulling tomato plants out of their flower beds and volunteer strawberries out of their asparagus patches, all for the sake of keeping some semblance of order in their gardens.

But weeding and controlling weeds are essential garden chores. While you can haul out the chemicals to kill weeds, your absolute best weapon is prevention. Follow some basic good garden practices and your weed population will be cut in half.

Don't let weeds get the upper hand. Keep your flower beds and vegetable gardens weeded. Be diligent in ripping out or chemically treating weeds like creeping charlie and dandelions when they're small, and you'll save yourself loads of problems later on. If weeding seems an overwhelming job, mark off a one-by-one-yard patch of your vegetable garden with sticks or string. Doing a small, defined area seems less daunting. And whatever you do, don't ever let weeds form seeds. One chickweed plant, for example, can produce thousands of seeds.

Mulch. Mulching not only prevents weeds, it conserves moisture. Mulch with grass clippings, pine needles, wood chips, shredded leaves, and just about any other organic matter. You can also mulch with gravel. Around shrubs and other permanent plantings, lay black landscaping fabric. It allows water to penetrate but smothers any weeds or weed seed underneath it and makes it tough for new weeds to take root on top of it. Layer at least two inches of mulch on top of the plastic. You can also use newspaper, but it will only last a few months. Layer about six layers of paper over the area you want to mulch. Cover with wood chips or another mulch to disguise the paper.

Weed when the soil is damp. After a good rain or a good watering is the best time to weed. You'll be able to get the long taproots of weeds, such as dandelions, which must have at least the top two inches of root removed to die. Weeds that spread by underground runners will also pull out more easily. Try one of the innovative weeding tools available, such as a stirrup hoe or a Cape Cod weeder.

Prevent weeds in lawns without herbicides by taking good care of the grass. Feed your lawn in the spring and fall (with an organic fertilizer, if you choose). Keep it mowed. Mowing not only keeps the grass looking good, it chops off small weeds. Watering an established lawn is less important for weed control, especially after July. Aerating the lawn every two or three years, using a machine you can rent, also creates unfavorable conditions for weeds that like compacted soil.

COMMON WEEDS

Chickweed. An annual. Easy to pull. Can hoe out while small. Don't leave lying in the garden or will reroot.

Clover. A perennial. Easy to pull or can hoe out. Can reroot if left lying in the garden.

Crabgrass. An annual. Prevented in lawns with a pre-emergent herbicide. Pull out of flower and vegetable gardens because when chopped with a hoe, some pieces can become new plants.

Dandelions. Perennials. Broadleaf herbicides kill these in lawns. Can pull individually, but get at least two inches of the taproot. Can hoe out very small plants.

Ground ivy. A perennial. Easy to pull. but can still return. Will reroot, however, if left lying around. If must treat with a herbicide, use Roundup or another nonselective type.

Knotweed. An annual. Thrives in compacted soil, so loosen the soil if possible. Easy to pull or hoe out young plants. Long taproot makes it tough to pull older plants, so use a hoe or dig out.

Plantain. A perennial. Thrives in compacted soil, so loosen the soil if possible. Can hoe out small plants. Hoe or dig out larger plants, getting as much of the plant as possible. Broadleaf herbicides can control this in lawns.

Quackgrass. A perennial. Dig out roots from under stems. Don't chop with a hoe, since new plants can grow from pieces.

Wild violets. Perennials. Dig out carefully from soft soil, taking care to get as much of the spreading roots as possible. A broadleaf herbicide controls these in lawns.

BEST CUT FLOWERS

ANNUALS

Celosia
Cleome
Cornflower
Cosmos
Larkspur
Marigolds
Salvia
Snapdragons
Zinnias

PERENNIALS

Artemisia
Asters
Astilbe
Baby's breath
Bee balm
Black-eyed Susan
Carnations
Chrysanthemum
Columbine

FLOWERS FOR CUTTING

Half the joy of flowers is bringing them indoors.

You don't need hours of flower-arranging classes to make a pretty bouquet for your dining-room table or front hall. All you really need is a container, water, and flowers.

A flower arrangement can be as simple as a single flower in a small vase or as elaborate as two dozen different types of flowers massed in a three-foot-high bouquet.

Good flower arrangements start with the flowers. Some flowers lend themselves to cutting better than others. Baby's breath, for example, will stay attractive in a vase for two weeks, while petunias will foul the water and smell bad after a day or two.

Cut flowers for an arrangement early in the morning or in the evening. Bring them indoors or to a cool, shady spot in the yard. Immediately condition them, that is, help them absorb as much water as possible by putting stems and leaves for a few hours in a tall, deep container in tepid water up to the flowers.

Select a container. You don't have to have a fancy vase. Ceramic bowls, teapots, crocks, coffee mugs, watering cans, drinking glasses, and just about any-thing else that's waterproof can be a vase. Try arranging flowers in jars or bowls and slipping the container into a wooden box or wicker basket. Collect containers for flower arranging at garage sales, junk shops, and discount stores on sale.

To prepare a flower for arrangement, remove it from the container of water. Strip off the lower leaves with your fingers. Cut to the desired length.

You can put all the flowers loose into a vase, especially if it has a narrow neck. But flower arranging is much easier with an anchor of some sort. At florists' shops or craft stores you can buy needlepoint holders, sometimes called frogs—little rounds with dozens of metal needles poking up. You can also purchase green floral foam, sometimes called Oasis. Cut a square of the foam, submerge it in warm water for five minutes, and put it in the container or vase. For a balanced arrangement, make sure the foam protrudes about one inch higher than the rim of the container. Fill the foam with flowers and foliage on both the top and the sides.

Experiment with arrangements you find pleasing. Study pictures of arrangements and bouquets from flower shops.

Use foliage as filler. Any green foliage, including that from your houseplants, can be used. Experienced flower arrangers grow more than just flowers that are good for cutting. They also grow plants that can provide good filler for their arrangements, including asparagus ferns, artemisia, baby's breath, coral bells, euphorbia, peonies, yarrow, and others.

Keep the arrangement well watered. Floral preservative, also available at florists' shops, will add days to the arrangement's life. Trimming the bottom of the stems every two or three days improves their ability to absorb water. You'll be able to enjoy your arrangement for several days.

PERENNIALS, CONT.

Coreopsis
Daffodils
Delphiniums
Euphorbia
Forsythia
Garden phlox
Goldenrod
Hydrangeas
Irises
Liatris
Lilacs
Lilies, Asiatic and Oriental
Lily-of-the-valley
Lythrum
Peonies
Perennial sunflower
Roses
Rue
Shasta daisy
Statice
Tulips
Yarrow

ORGANIC GARDENING

Over the past twenty years, gardeners have shown an increased interest in gardening without chemicals.

Certainly, there still are gardeners who treat their lawns, vegetables, flowers, and trees with a variety of chemicals with no qualms. They yearn for the good old days when you could blast night crawlers with chlordane, now outlawed because it was found to have a harmful effect on the environment. Now there are no ways to control night crawlers, though they do improve the quality of the soil. Still, that's little comfort to those who watch their manicured lawns become bumpy and loaded with tiny dirt mounds.

At the other extreme are those gardeners profoundly concerned about the effects of chemicals on themselves and their environment. Even when a chemical is shown to be safe and is approved by the Environmental Protection Agency, these gardeners would prefer to be safer and not sorry. They use absolutely no chemicals of any kind.

The vast majority of gardeners fall somewhere in the middle. They try to follow tried-and-true organic gardening methods because they know they work and they aren't expensive. They compost because it's effec-

tive. They try to prevent the need for chemically eradicating insects and diseases by practicing good gardening techniques that keep their plants healthy and therefore disease resistant. But when creeping charlie again threatens to take over their shady backyards, they bring in the Roundup.

Think carefully about which gardening practices you want to follow, read up on organic gardening, and read all labels with a critical eye. There are few right or wrong ways to garden. But especially when it comes to chemicals, all gardeners should thoughtfully follow the garden practices they feel are best for themselves and those around them.

To make your own intelligent decisions about how you'll use chemicals in your garden, ask yourself the following questions.

How much plant loss and disease are you willing to tolerate? If an infestation of whiteflies in your vegetable garden and the resulting partial loss of produce or flowers doesn't bother you, you're a good candidate for completely organic gardening. However, if you don't want to give up a single plant to insects or disease, reconsider. You might want to rely on chemicals at least as a last resort.

How much work are you willing to do? While many organic gardening practices take no more time—or even less time—than more chemically oriented practices, organic gardening does demand certain tasks and resources. Manure is the best fertilizer around, but are you willing to find a manure source of your own or lug in several bags of composted manure from the garden center? One reason chemical gardening caught on after World War II was that it was cheap and easy and didn't require much thought. Organic gardening requires research and lots of thought. The payoffs, however, are healthy plants that are as chemically free as possible.

How do you define "organic"? Capitalizing on the popularity of organic gardening, many garden supply companies are doing all they can to market their products as organic. It can be confusing. A nursery, for example, might carry liquid copper sulfate in a display of "organic" supplies. But right on the label, the manufacturer warns that copper sulfate should be kept out of the reach of children and handled with great care and that significant amounts of copper sulfate in water can kill fish. That doesn't sound very organic. Other gardeners seem to think that if it comes out of the kitchen, it must be organic. But dishwashing soap, a popular component of many organic insect sprays, may well not be biodegradeable and may not be phosphate free.

TIP

Paint the handle of all your tools a bright color, such as red. It makes trowels, hoes, and other garden tools much easier to find among the plants and grass.

FLORENCE
VANDER MEIDEN,
PELLA GARDEN CLUB

FALL CROPS

Fall is not the time to put a garden to bed.

Granted, some tender plants, such as tomatoes and peppers, are on the wane. But others, such as broccoli, lettuces, kale, and spinach, are just approaching their peak.

With careful planning, in the fall you will have a second harvest of cool-loving vegetables from the garden.

Late July and early August is the time to get a start on your fall vegetable garden. Vegetables that thrive in cool weather and can be sown from seed directly in the ground include peas, radishes, mustard greens, kale, Swiss chard, turnips, rutabagas, lettuces, and spinach.

To harvest lettuces and spinach early, use this trick: start them in pots or flats in a cool, shady place. The containers make it easier to give them the black soil (preferably potting soil) they like. The shade makes it easier to keep them watered. Transplant into the garden when they're an inch high.

You can also grow cabbage, broccoli, Brussels sprouts, and cauliflower by planting the seedlings in the ground now. You can buy seedlings this time of year at better-stocked greenhouses. Or you can start your own in early June in containers and transplant them into the garden the first week of August.

Plant the seeds and seedlings in your best, blackest, most moisture-retentive garden soil. Keep them well watered. Come October, you'll be delighting in the fruits of your labor.

SEPTEMBER CHECKLIST

🌾 Expect the first frost around September 30 in northern Iowa and October 15 in southern Iowa. Tender plants can be protected from the first few frosts by covering them with sheets, blankets, or other protective material.

🌾 If you're using lawn chemicals, apply fertilizer and broadleaf control this month. You can buy them in a two-in-one package known as a "weed and feed" combination.

🌾 Plant spring-flowering bulbs later in the month or in very early October.

🌾 Plant lilies, such as tiger, Oriental, and Asiatic, this month.

🌾 Dig dahlias, tuberous begonias, caladiums, gladiolus, and cannas later this month. Cure in a warm room, and store covered with perlite or vermiculite in a very cool place (about forty-five degrees).

🌾 Plant evergreens, as long as they're balled-and-burlapped or in containers, this month.

🌾 If you're not going to protect them in some way, harvest eggplants, peppers, and tomatoes before the first frost. These plants and other flowers and tender plants can be protected from the first few frosts by throwing a sheet, blanket, tarp, or other cover over them. To protect vegetables for a few more weeks, secure Reemay or other superlight spun cloth on the top with clips and/or string.

🌾 The first two weeks of September is a good time to plant perennials or to divide and transplant perennials you already have.

🌾 Reseed lawns early in the month. Keep the soil moist until the seeds sprout. Sod lawns anytime this month through October.

Rake leaves. Leaving them on the lawn can kill the grass. Don't worry about leaves that have collected around your shrubs. If you don't mind their looks, they'll actually protect the plant. You can greatly diminish the volume of the leaves (and create a terrific mulch) by mowing over the leaves with your power mower with a bag attached. You can even mow the lawn and collect leaves in an easy one-step process.

Keep dead or diseased foliage and spent blooms trimmed. Give up altogether on diseased annuals. Don't put them on your compost heap, or they'll have the potential to spread disease.

After frost begins killing flowers and vegetables, remove them. (Some plants are more tender and will succumb earlier than others.) Annuals can simply be ripped out by their roots. Perennials (but not roses) should be cut one or two inches off the ground with pruning shears.

Mulch cut-off perennials with straw, wood chips, pine needles or boughs, shredded leaves, or any other handy organic matter.

COLD FRAMES

You can have lettuce through Thanksgiving with the help of a simple, inexpensive gardening device: the cold frame.

Even beginning gardeners should experiment with one. A cold frame will let you harvest radishes, lettuces, spinach, and other crops six weeks later (and in the spring, six weeks earlier) than your neighbors. Cold frames are not complicated—they're nothing more than a bottomless box with a transparent top that works like a minigreenhouse. (When a method of heating the frame, such as heating cables laid on the soil, is added, it's called a hotbed.)

You can buy cold frame kits through gardening catalogs, but it's far cheaper and very easy to build your own.

To build a cold frame, first find something to use as the top. This can be an old storm window, scrounged from the garage or bought dirt-cheap at a garage sale or junk shop, a sheet of transparent fiberglass from the hardware store, or any other piece of flat, transparent material. You can also stretch heavy-duty clear plastic over a wooden frame of pine laths and staple the plastic down. Lightweight tops will need to be held on top of the cold frame with bricks or otherwise fastened down to prevent them from blowing off.

For the sides of the frame, nail together with galvanized nails pressure-treated pine, untreated cedar, or scrap lumber to fashion a four-sided box the length and width of the top. The lumberyard will cut boards to your specifications if you don't have a saw.

If you want to get fancy, you can cut two triangular pieces the width of the box to automatically slant the top toward the sun. Or simply bury the front of your box deeper than the back so that the top is tilted toward the south or southwest. Tilting the top assures maximum sunlight and warmth in the cold frame.

Attach the horizontal boards to each other with one-by-two-inch pine laths, nailed vertically across the boards.

Make sure the soil in which you place the cold frame is good, fertile soil that is well drained. Work the soil with a spade or spading fork, adding plenty of compost.

Once the cold frame is installed, plant quick-growing crops that like cool weather. They should be compact plants since your cold frame has limited space. Good candidates include lettuce, spinach, radishes, mustard, Swiss chard, and collard greens. Plant them in the soil according to seed package directions.

Water lightly and place the lid on top.

Monitor the cold frame carefully. On warm, sunny days, you may have to remove the lid partly or fully to make sure it doesn't get too hot. Placing a thermometer in the cold frame is helpful. Always cover the frame again in the very late afternoon or at sundown. On chilly nights, throw an old blanket over the cold frame to retain heat.

To reduce your work and worry, you can hinge the top of the cold frame. Automatic temperature-sensitive closers and openers are available through garden supply catalogs.

With a little luck, you'll be eating your cold frame vegetables in just a few weeks and can continue to harvest them until early winter.

After the last fall harvest from your cold frame, you can use it to store pots of bulbs planted to bloom indoors during early winter. Simply pot up the bulbs in November, water well, and store in the cold frame stuffed with straw or dead leaves. Check the pots every few weeks. When shoots start to poke out of the tops of the pots, bring indoors and place by a sunny window.

In the spring, the soil in the cold frame will warm up far earlier than the rest of the garden. Use it to plant fast-growing vegetables for early harvest or to nurture tomato plants or other tender vegetables and perennials until the last frost date is past, usually mid-May in Iowa.

TIP

Mulch newly planted bulbs, such as daffodils and tulips, and place a marker nearby so you don't accidentally disturb them.
IMA HEARN,
INDEPENDENCE
GARDEN CLUB

FORCING BULBS

You can brighten the worst winter day with brilliant yellow daffodils, scarlet tulips, or intensely fragrant purple hyacinths. All it takes is a handful of bulbs, some soil, and a lot of patience.

Forcing bulbs—the process of making spring flowers bloom in pots indoors during the winter—is surprisingly easy. All you do is plant bulbs in pots, chill them in a refrigerator or unheated garage to replicate winter, then place them in a sunny spot and watch spring happen inside your house.

Hyacinths force especially well. You can even buy a little forcing jar to fill with water and a hyacinth bulb. Crocuses, tulips, standard and miniature daffodils, and miniature irises also force well. Some varieties force better than others. Suppliers often note which ones force well in the bulb display or description.

Buy enough bulbs to arrange in one layer near the top of the container, with the sides of the bulbs almost touching. That usually means five or six tulip bulbs in a standard six-inch pot. Plant just one variety per pot because different bulbs have different blooming times.

Nearly any sort of container may be used if it has a hole in the bottom for drainage. Regular flowerpots work well, but special forcing bowls are available. You can use inexpensive plastic flowerpots, also.

Put a few pieces of broken flowerpots or a layer of gravel or stones in the bottom of the pot to promote good drainage. Nearly fill the pot with soil. Arrange the bulbs in a layer with pointed tips up. They should almost touch each other. Barely cover with soil.

When you're done, the bulbs' tips should just poke out of the soil, and the soil level should be a half inch below the rim.

Water the pots well. Put them in the refrigerator or in an attached garage where the temperatures are very cool but not freezing. Put a paper bag or cardboard box over the pots to keep them in the dark. (Do not wrap in plastic.)

Check the soil every few days, and water if it's dry when you put your finger a half inch into the soil. A white mildew may form on the soil, but it won't injure the bulbs. In eight to twelve weeks, pale shoots should emerge. Roots may also be pushing through the drainage hole.

Once the shoots are an inch high, move the pot to a warm and very sunny spot. Provide plenty of light or the plants will get leggy and flop over. The shoots will begin to green and grow. In a matter of a few weeks, your bulbs will begin to bloom. When it's time to display the bulbs, stick the plastic pot in a wicker basket and arrange dried Spanish moss around the pot to conceal the plastic.

Experienced gardeners like to stagger the potting of the bulbs and their removal from the cold over two or three months so that they have blooms throughout the winter.

Opinions vary about what to do with the bulbs after blooming. Some people report success with keeping the dying bulbs well watered and planting them outdoors in the spring. Others recommend simply pitching them.

Forcing bulbs isn't hard. For a few minutes' work in the fall, you'll be thanking yourself in January, when your home is filled with brilliantly blooming flowers.

TIP

If deer are a problem in your garden, plant daffodils and forget tulips. Deer relish tulips but won't touch daffodils.
ARLEEN TROESTER, COLESBURG GARDEN CLUB

Bringing Plants Indoors

If you've ever winced while writing a check at the greenhouse, consider saving your tender plants from year to year.

Many plants that other gardeners buy again and again each spring can be dug up from the garden in the fall and brought indoors. Good candidates for overwintering in your home include geraniums, heliotrope, wax begonias, impatiens, New Guinea impatiens, rosemary, coleus, and ornamental peppers. Experiment with your own favorite annuals.

To bring a plant indoors, carefully dig it up by the roots. Put it in the largest pot practical and fill with potting soil, not ordinary garden soil. Supply as much light as possible, such as that from a south-facing window or grow light.

The plants will look good for the first couple of months and then will start to look ratty. Keep them well watered, and fertilize very lightly two or three times during the winter. Trim off any dying or diseased foliage. Keep blooms pinched off.

Keep an eye out for insect infestations. Spider mites, for example, love the warm, dry conditions indoors. If you see signs of an insect problem, wrap the pot and soil in aluminum foil or a plastic bag. Dunk the foliage into warm, soapy water and swish around. Rinse in cool water. If that doesn't work, try one of the many insecticides (some of which are organic) available at garden centers.

During the first pleasant days of spring, place the plants outdoors. Leave them outdoors as much as possible, but don't expose them to temperatures below forty degrees. They should start to regain their vigor and send out healthy new growth. Plant in the ground after May 15.

In the fall, you can also take cuttings from plants to root indoors. A few plants, such as coleus, can be rooted simply by cutting off four-inch ends, stripping the bottom two inches of their leaves, and sticking in a jar of water in a sunny window. Pot when the root is about one-half-inch long.

Others plants should be cut off and stripped of their leaves in the same manner. But instead of putting them in water, where they would rot, dip their cut ends in rooting hormone. Stick in a small pot filled with damp perlite. Keep damp, and in two or three weeks a root system will develop. After about a month, transplant into a pot filled with potting soil. Keep in a sunny window or under a grow light. Plant outdoors in mid-May.

OCTOBER

OCTOBER CHECKLIST

The first frost in Iowa is usually in early to mid October.

BEFORE THE FROST:

❧ To prolong the harvest season, for the first few frosts, cover vegetables with old sheets and blankets. Remove during the day. For longer term protection from frost, cover with spun-bond garden fabric, sold by garden suppliers under various brand names, including Reemay. It can be left on indefinitely because it lets in sun and water. Don't cover kale or Brussels sprouts, however. They taste better after a frost.

❧ In the vegetable garden the first week of October, plant a cover crop, such as winter rye. Keep watered until it germinates. Till it under in the spring to greatly improve your soil.

❧ Dig up any annuals or other tender plants—such as gladiolus, cannas, dahlias, and caladiums—that you want to save over the winter.

❧ Plant spring-blooming bulbs in early October.

❧ Store leftover garden seed in its packets in a tightly sealed glass jar in the refrigerator. If you like, wrap one tablespoon powdered milk powder in a tissue to serve as a desiccant.

❧ On a clear, dry day, pick flowers and any remaining herbs for drying.

❧ Fall is an excellent time for creating a new flower or vegetable bed (see pages 26–27). If possible, plant it with a cover crop to improve the soil. In the spring, simply till it under and you're ready to plant.

❧ If you want to continue to harvest root vegetables, such as carrots, leeks, and celeriac, through the early winter, cover them while still in the ground with eight to ten inches of straw or hay. Mark so that you'll be able to find the spot even under a few feet of snow. Later on, simply dig up the vegetables and use as usual.

If you're going to harvest lettuces, spinach, and other cool-loving vegetables through the winter, cover early in the month with hoops and plastic to protect from the cold.

Instead of leaving root crops in the ground, you can also dig them up. Allow vegetables such as potatoes and onions to cure for two weeks in a shady, well-ventilated place, such as a porch, spread out in a single layer on newspapers. Store in a cool, but not cold, dry place. Carrots can be stored covered with damp sand.

AFTER THE FROST:

Leave asparagus foliage standing over the winter.

Empty pots and window boxes after the plants in them die. Leaving ceramic or terra-cotta pots out over the winter will make them crack and break.

Continue to rake leaves. If you don't want to compost them, try digging them into your vegetable garden. Whole leaves will at least partially break down and chopped leaves will almost completely break down by spring and enrich the soil.

As the frost kills plants, remove them. Annuals should be dug up or pulled out by their roots. Perennials, except for roses, should be cut off an inch or two above ground. Put undiseased plant material in a compost pile, chopping up large pieces. If plant material is diseased, put it on a special, separate pile to prevent disease from spreading.

Turn your compost pile a couple of times a month, if possible.

Water young shrubs and trees if the fall is dry.

FALL-BLOOMING PLANTS

In October, everything seems to be dying. But in a carefully planned garden, you can expect a final burst of bloom in the autumn before the first snows hit.

The color of turning trees, especially maples, is usually the star of the fall garden. But there are a number of shrubs and perennials to plant specifically because of the welcome color they provide during the fall.

Burning bush is a fall favorite because of its seemingly flaming red leaves. Mums, asters, and sedum "Autumn Joy" are also commonly planted for their fall color. Some plants produce beautiful fruits in the fall. Bittersweet, which is a vine, is a prime example.

There are many other less commonly grown plants that do very well in Iowa. Autumn crocus, for example, provides a surprising bit of color poking through the fallen leaves.

Still other plants are planted for their summer color but put on a subtle fall show. Lythrum, for ex-ample, sends up lovely purple-pink spires in the summer, which fade by late summer. In the fall, the tiny leaves on the four-foot plants become slightly translucent and turn every shade between gold and amber. Even the foliage of the much-planted daylily, a perennial favored for its July display of flowers, turns a deep gold that plays off the browns and reds and other fall colors around it.

Fall gardens have a different kind of beauty. In summer, the bright colors of blossoms compete with their neighbors. In the fall, you'll have to settle, perhaps, for the tawny forms of drying ornamental grasses or the satisfaction of the papery bark of a bare birch.

To plan a better fall garden, take walks around your neighborhood, public parks, arboretums, and landscape or garden centers to get ideas. Take note of what's at its prime and what would fit in your garden. Browse through the mail-order catalogs, too.

Plants with Fall Color

SHRUBS AND VINES

American bittersweet (*Celastrus scandens*). 20 feet. Full sun. A very vigorous vine that can strangle a small tree if not controlled. Probably the best of the bittersweets. Must plant two for pollination. Beautiful fruits in fall.

Blackhaw virburnum (*Virburnum prunifolium*). Deep red leaves.

Bluebeard or blue spiraea (*Caryopteris × clandonensis*). 3 feet. Full sun. Blue flowers in fall. Hardy in Zone 5.

Burning bush (*Euonymus*). 12 feet. Full sun. Best-known cultivars are bright red. Some produce clear gold leaves and crimson fruits in October.

Dwarf amur maple (*Acer ginnala* "Compactum"). 8 feet. Full sun. Excellent red to wine color.

Korean barberry (*Berberis koreana*). 5 feet. Full sun. Excellent bright red color.

Sea buckthorn (*Hippophae rhamnoides*). 15 feet. Full sun. Bright orange fruit a quarter inch in size.

Smokebush (*Cotinus coggyria*). 15 feet. Full sun. Leaves turn yellow to purple.

Spreading cotoneaster (*Cotoneaster divaricata*). 6 feet. Full sun. Outstanding fluorescent red, yellow, and purple fall color.

Staghorn sumac, smooth sumac, flame sumac (*Rhus*). 24 feet. Full sun. Excellent color varying from yellow to brilliant red. Can also be pruned into a tree.

Sweet autumn clematis (*Clematis paniculata*). 25 feet. Full sun to partial shade. August–October. A vine. Very fragrant white flowers. Plumy white fruits produced late is season.

Witch hazel (*Hamamelis virginiana*). 12 feet. Full sun. Nice yellow color with tiny, fragrant yellow flowers.

PERENNIALS

Aster. 3–6 feet. Full sun. September–October. Many varieties in many colors.

Boltonia. 4–6 feet. Full sun. August–September. White or pink flowers. Closely resemble asters.

Chinese-lantern or ground cherry (*Physalis alkekengi*). 2 feet. Full sun. September–November. Bright orange fruitlike calyces that make good cut flowers.

Chrysanthemum. 2 feet. Full sun. October–November. Range of fall colors including yellow, maroon, gold, purple, and white. Very reliable.

Double thinleaf sunflower or pale sunflower (*Helianthus decapetalus*). 4 feet. Full sun. August–September. Large yellow flowers.

Giant daisy (*Chrysanthemum serotinum*). 5 feet. Full sun. August–September. Daisylike flowers.

Obedience plant (*Physostegia virginiana*). 2 feet. Full sun to partial shade. September. White or bright pink flowers.

Pitcher sage (*Salvia azurea* Grandiflora). 5 feet. Full sun. August–September. Deep blue flowers. Not reliably hardy in Zone 4.

Sedum "Autumn Joy." 2 feet. Full sun to partial shade. August–October. Deep rose flowers.

Sneezeweed (*Helenium autumnale*). 5 feet. Full sun. August–September. Yellow or red flowers.

Windflower (*Anemone japonica* or *Anemone* × *hybrida*). 2 feet. Partial shade to full sun. September–November. White or pink flowers.

BULBS

Autumn crocus (*Colchicum autumnale*). 4 feet. Full sun to partial shade. August–September. Purple flowers. Very poisonous.

Henry lily (*Lilium henryi*). 8 feet. Partial shade. August–September. Soft orange flowers.

Tiger lily (*Lilium tigrinum*). 2–5 feet. Full sun to partial shade. July–September. Orange and other-colored flowers bloom from July to September, according to the variety.

NOVEMBER

NOVEMBER CHECKLIST

🌿 Mulch strawberries before the temperature drops below twenty degrees. Do not use grass clippings or leaves. They mat down and suffocate the plants. Instead, use straw, sawdust, or any other light mulch. You may want to put large branches or kindling on top of the mulch to hold it in place.

🌿 Roses should already be mounded with dirt. Protect canes with burlap or other materials. When possible, don't prune until early spring.

🌿 If you want to force an amaryllis to bloom, plant the bulb in a six- or seven-inch pot. Let upper third of bulb remain above the soil line. Water and set in a cool, dim location. Keep moist. Leaves will appear in about four weeks. At that time, set in a sunny spot.

🌿 Mulch perennials and other landscape plants for winter protection. Pine boughs are nearly ideal, but straw, shredded leaves, pine needles, and other materials also work well.

🌿 Mowers and other large, power garden tools should be taken in to be serviced. Have the mower blade sharpened to prevent browning of the grass tips next spring. Check out the snowblower, too, to make sure it's in shape for the first snow.

🌿 Clean sprayers and garden tools. Take them in to be sharpened or repaired or do so yourself. Rub them lightly with oil to prevent rusting.

- Prevent rabbit and rodent damage to young trees and shrubs, particularly fruit trees, by making a collar about two or three feet high from wire mesh. Bury the bottom about three inches into the soil.

- Check any vegetables you've stored for spoilage. Remove damaged vegetables immediately.

- Keep forced bulbs well watered.

- Keep an eye on plants growing outdoors in plant tunnels or in a cold frame. On very cold nights, throw an old blanket or sleeping bag over the cold frame.

Cut old stockings lengthwise to make ties for tomato plants, cauliflower, and many other plants. These will not cut into the stalk and are very strong. Cut several now while gardening chores are few and store until spring.

NITA LARSON AND
THE SHELBY COUNTY
FEDERATED
GARDEN CLUB

COMPOST

It's not for nothing that compost is called a gardener's "black gold."

Compost, the best of which looks like black, crumbly dirt, does just about everything. Worked into the soil, it feeds plants, helps the soil retain water, makes weeds easier to pull, and prevents plant disease by creating a better growing environment. A compost pile is an absolute must for every garden. Not only is it wonderful for plants, it's the best sort of trash bin. Grass clippings, vegetable and fruit scraps, leaves, small sticks, fireplace ashes, eggshells, coffee grounds, dead plant material, weeds and frost-killed annuals all can be dumped onto the compost heap. (Just don't put on any meat products or animal waste from animals that eat meat.) A compost heap is far easier and cheaper than bagging all that stuff up. Despite popular myth, a compost heap doesn't have a strong smell unless you add manure.

Your compost pile can be as simple as a plain old pile with no sides out behind the garage. Throw a few pieces of firewood or branches on top to prevent the materials from blowing away. It can be as elaborate as a specially made bin lined with black plastic to create optimal conditions for the plants to decompose.

To create a compost pile, you have two choices. The first, a cold-rot pile, is the easiest. Just dump all your organic plant material in a pile. You can surround the pile with concrete blocks, wire fencing, or a specially made compost bin available at greenhouses and hardware stores, but it's not essential. Some people simply dig a hole in the ground for a compost pit. If you like, turn the pile occasionally with a pitchfork. Or give it a soaking with a hose in dry weather. The center of the pile will get warm but not hot.

After about a year, the bottom of the pile will have several inches of black, crumbly compost. It will still have chunks of orange peel or a corn stalk here and there, but you can just pull those out.

For a more scientific, hot-rot compost pile, layer "wet" and "dry" materials. The most readily available wet materials are grass clippings and manure of plant-eating animals, such as sheep, cattle, and horses. Autumn leaves are the most available dry material.

In the autumn, save fallen leaves in plastic bags over the winter. In the spring, after your first lawn mowing, collect grass clippings. Dump a bag or two of the leaves in the compost pile, and put half the grass clippings on top. Put another bag or two of leaves on the clippings, and top with the remaining grass clippings. Water well. Turn every three or four days, and keep damp. You'll have compost in a matter of weeks.

If possible, collect clippings from neighbors who haven't treated their lawns with herbicides. Layer those with your saved leaves. Water well and water once a week thereafter, unless you get a good rain.

You can really speed up the composting process by adding fresh manure between the layers of grass and leaves. It makes the compost a better fertilizer.

The center of the pile will get quite hot. So hot, in fact, that if you put your hand in the middle of the pile, it will be just a little too hot to leave in for more than a few moments.

Compost can be spread on flower beds, and put in flowerpots and window boxes. No matter how fast you make compost, however, you'll find that you can never have too much of this very good thing.

🌿 🌿 **TIP** 🌿 🌿

To discourage the use of your plants, including houseplants, as a cat litter box, cut a slit and a hole in the middle of a pie tin and place it around the base of the plant.
KATHLEEN MOENCH,
BUSINESS WOMEN'S
GARDEN CLUB,
DES MOINES

Annual statice
Bachelor's-buttons
Celosia
Globe amaranth
Larkspur
Lemon verbena
Pot marigolds
Salvia farinacea
Strawflower
Yellow marigolds
Zinnias

Artemesia
Chrysanthemums
German statice
Large and miniature roses
Lavender
Peonies
White candytuft
Yarrow

DRIED FLOWERS

You can carry the pleasures of the garden into the winter by drying flowers. Dried flowers can be arranged in vases, formed into wreaths, or, with the addition of scented oil, transformed into potpourri.

There are several ways to dry flowers. To use in vases, simply cut the flowers at their prime throughout the summer. Strip off leaves and tie into small bunches. Hang upside down in an airy closet or garage.

You can dry flowers whole with silica, available at florists' shops. Spread an even layer of silica in an airtight container. Arrange whole flowers upright with the stem removed. Gently spread another layer of silica over them to cover. Cover with an airtight lid. Check every few days until the flowers are entirely dry, usually in a week or two. (Use wire stems, available at craft stores, when arranging.)

If you need petals for potpourri, dry the flowers by spreading them on a cookie sheet lined with paper towels. Leave in a warm, well-ventilated area out of direct light, such as the dark corner of a garage, on top of the refrigerator under a cabinet, or in an open paper bag.

Arrange dried flowers in a vase, wooden box, or basket. Using a block of dried Oasis, the green foam florists use, simplifies the process of arranging the flowers. Or purchase an Oasis wreath at a craft store. Fill the wreath with dried flowers. Bittersweet, a vine, can simply be twisted while fresh into a wreath and allowed to dry in that shape. If you use a straw wreath, you can attach the dried flowers with floral wire, floral tape, or a hot glue gun.

Your dried flower crafts will last longer if you spray them with a fixative made specifically for dried flowers. The fixative is available at craft centers and florists' shops.

Making your own fragrant potpourri is easy. All it takes are some dried plant materials, oil, and chopped orris root.

Chopped orris root can be found or ordered at pharmacies. You can use powdered orris root in a pinch, but it will give the potpourri a slightly dusty appearance. You can also order potpourri supplies through the mail (see pages 136–139).

Fragrant oils can be found at craft supply stores in tiny vials. Like perfumes, very cheap oils have an artificial scent. High-quality oils smell very much like the actual plant.

Make potpourri by placing three tablespoons of chopped orris root in a quart jar or other sealable glass or ceramic container. Do not let metal come in contact with the potpourri. It affects the fragrance. Add a half teaspoon of scented oil, and stir with a wooden spoon or chopstick. Cover tightly, and set aside for three days. Shake once each day.

After three days, pour the orris root–oil mixture into a large glass or ceramic bowl. Add three to four cups dried plant material, and toss very gently. Put in a glass jar, and seal lid tightly. Toss lightly every two or three days. After two weeks, it should have a strong scent. If not, add another half teaspoon of oil. Continue to toss lightly every two or three days until the scent is strong.

Display the potpourri in baskets or in ceramic and glass bowls (not metal—it reacts with the potpourri), or make tiny sachets tied with a ribbon to tuck into drawers and closets. You can revive the scent after a few weeks by tossing the potpourri with several drops of brandy.

FLOWERS TO DRY, CONT.

OTHER

Autumn leaves
Bits of fresh evergreen
Bittersweet
Cattails
Cedar chips
Decorative grass plumes and blades
Dried berries from holly and firethorn shrubs
Tiny pine cones

DECEMBER

DECEMBER CHECKLIST

🌿 Keep poinsettias well watered in a bright spot away from extremes of heat and cold.

🌿 Put ashes from your fireplace on the compost heap.

🌿 Use calcium chloride rather than sodium chloride on your walks to melt ice. Salt hurts plants.

🌿 Toss snow—as long as it doesn't have salt in it—from your driveway and walks onto perennial beds to protect them.

🌿 Recycle your Christmas tree by cutting off the branches and laying them over your perennial beds as a winter mulch. If you have a chipper, shred the tree. If you live in the country or on a large lot, leave the tree in an out-of-sight spot for wildlife cover.

🌿 Don't fertilize houseplants this month.

🌿 Place orders for special seed and plant catalogs.

🌿 Catch up on garden reading.

🌿 Rest. Early winter is one of the few times gardeners can sit back and take a breather from their warmer weather chores.

🌿 You can still harvest Brussels sprouts from the garden. You can also harvest root vegetables you protected with straw.

🌿 Keep any bulbs you're forcing and plants under an artificial light and well watered.

🌿 Evaluate your winter landscaping. Think of ways to hide unattractive winter spots, highlight visually appealing areas, or include plants with winter interest in your garden. Take notes to use in the spring when planting.

Winter Gardens

On a cold December day, take a look out your window. What do you see? Too many gardeners see the ratty remains of last summer's flowers, garbage cans, and their neighbor's garage. Others, however, see a carefully planned planting of evergreens, trees with interesting forms and barks, bright red berries, and a variety of birds and wildlife. The best yards don't just look good in June; they even look good in deepest winter.

Especially in Iowa, it makes sense to garden with winter landscaping in mind. We do, after all, spend a lot of time blanketed in cold, snow, and ice. We might as well make the most of it.

Winter should be considered in your overall garden plan. The most obvious way to do this is to plant evergreens. Evergreens can shield the view of your neighbor's garbage can or dog run, soften the corners of your house, hide and soften the foundation of your home, and provide a pleasant focal point in your yard. An evergreen hedge is softer, and usually less expensive, than a fence. It provides year-round privacy and is a superb backdrop for flowers in summer.

Don't rely on the old standbys, plain junipers and pines. Try holly (those varieties that are hardy enough for Iowa) or red barberry. Some evergreens, like the American arborvitae "Rheingold" and the spreading juniper "Mother Lode," have gorgeous yellow foliage that turns bronze or yellow-bronze in the winter. *Thuja occidentalis* "Emerald" has a naturally aristocratic, upright form that flanks gates and doorways beautifully. Covered with snow, well-planned evergreens look like a picture on a Christmas card.

A note on evergreens: don't trim them mercilessly. With the exception of a well-trimmed hedge, those tight little balls and boxes that too many people whack their evergreens into are stiff and unflattering to the landscape. Unless you have a French formal garden or are a topiary artist, you're probably better off following the shrubs' loose, natural form. Just give the shrubs and trees a light annual trim that keeps them in bounds. Don't trim all the branches to the same length. Let some poke out a little, while others are shorter. The best-pruned evergreens look like no one prunes them at all.

When planning your garden for winter, look for plants with interesting barks and forms. Red-twigged dogwood is a popular shrub in Iowa that, true to its name, has bright red bark that stands out against the snow. *Salix alba* "Britzensis," commonly called coral embers willow, has stunning orange-red branches

When leaving on vacation, keep potted plants healthy by watering well and covering them with a clear dry-cleaning bag. The plants will stay watered for up to three weeks.

DARLENE LORENZ,
INDEPENDENCE
GARDEN CLUB

that stand out when planted in front of evergreens.

When choosing rose bushes, look for those with bright, berrylike hips. Many shrubs, such as holly and some varieties of viburnum, bear berries that last throughout the winter. *Ilex verticillata* "Winter Red" is a type of holly that has beautiful red berries in the winter and should be hardy in southern Iowa. Many hollies are not hardy throughout the state.

Other plants with winter interest can be incorporated into your landscape. Sedum "Autumn Joy" left standing through the winter is lovely. Tall grasses, such as pampas grass, are attractive in late fall through late winter and are particularly pretty with a covering of frost.

Don't discount the role of benches, statues, arbors, and other garden accents and structures. A bench with a dusting of snow is quietly beautiful. The bee skep that was half hidden in the border in July will now be a simple focal point. When choosing accessories for your garden, consider their role in the winter landscape as well as that of summer.

Wildlife is another important aspect of winter gardening. Providing a bird bath (with a heater to keep away the ice) attracts birds. Bird feeders also help. Match the type of feeder and feed with the type of bird you wish to attract. A platform feeder, a sort of large wooden platter on a three- or four-foot post filled with mixed seed, will attract a wide variety of birds and is easy to make yourself. Or try hanging a suet ball on a tree outside your favorite window.

You'll find that there's more happening in a winter garden than you might at first think.

GIFTS FROM THE GARDEN

Gifts from your garden are among the most personal and thoughtful you could find. The garden that was so bountiful in the summer can continue to give into December. Here are some ideas.

Seed greeting cards. Gather seeds from your garden in late summer (see pages 71–72). Put them in tiny, handmade paper packets, seal with tape, and label. You can also use the clear-plastic self-sealing packets used by jewelers. Tuck them into your holiday greeting cards for a special touch. While you're at it, you might even feature your garden in your cards. Take winterscape photos of your garden or shots of bright red flowers during the summer; then turn them into greeting cards.

Potpourris and sachets. Save flower petals and fragrant herbs through the summer to make potpourri (see pages 114–115). Wrap in a decorative paper bag, or make small cloth bags to stuff with potpourri. Tie with a ribbon for a sachet to perfume drawers.

Preserved produce. Brighten winter tables with gifts that burst with the freshness of summer. Fruit preserves, your special spaghetti sauce made with your own Italian tomatoes and homegrown herbs, and pesto are longtime favorites. These can be canned or frozen in jars and other containers. Label with a decorative label, and tie a ribbon on the container.

Homemade spices and herbs. Save dried herbs from the summer, and crush them well. For packages, make white paper packets labeled with your best handwriting. Or give them in tiny glass containers purchased at craft shops.

Forced bulbs. Whether in full bloom or just starting to poke shoots out of the soil, forced bulbs make ideal gifts (see pages 100–101). Force them in a pretty pot, and tie a red ribbon around the pot.

Garden certificates. Make a certificate promising garden help during the growing season—mowing lawns, trimming a hedge, creating a perennial bed. Tie to an inexpensive trowel.

Potted plants. If you've potted up cuttings or plant slips from your garden and they're still attractive, they'll make welcome gifts. An assortment of herbs, especially, makes a nice windowsill garden.

Herbal teas. If you like to grow herbs, dry the leaves of those that make good teas, such as camomile and the mints. Box in pretty tins.

Compost. An offbeat gift for the serious gardener. Save and sift your best compost. Store in one of those large tins popcorn comes in. It's great indoors for potting houseplants.

TIP

To avoid using insecticides, both on indoor and outdoor plants, spray them with a strong, steady stream of water.
CONNIE STAPLES,
BUSINESS WOMEN'S
GARDEN CLUB,
DES MOINES

RESOURCES

Best bulbs and perennials for Iowa

Achillea ptarmica (yarrow). 2 feet. Full sun. June–August. Yellow and white flowers. Good cut flower and dries very well. Very easy, drought resistant, and tolerates poor soil.

Althea rosea (hollyhock). 5 feet. Full sun. June–July. All colors but blue. A reliable, old-fashioned biennial (blooms the second year) that reseeds so freely it's treated as a perennial. Sometimes needs staking. Easy.

Anemone cylindrica or *Anemone* × *hybrida* (in varieties) (windflower). 2 feet. Partial shade. September–November. White or pink flowers. A good cut flower. Does best in northeast Iowa.

Aquilegia × varieties (columbine). 2.5 feet. Partial shade to sun. May–June. Many different colors. Good cut flower. Plant different colors at least 50 feet apart so they won't cross breed.

Asclepias tuberosa (butterfly milkweed). 2 feet. Full sun. July–August. Bright orange or yellow flowers attract butterflies. An Iowa native, it is drought tolerant. Very easy.

Aster (in varieties). 3–6 feet. Full sun. September–October. Many varieties, but mainly blue and bright pink. Excellent cut flowers. Easy.

Begonia (tuberous hybrids) (tuberous begonias). 1 foot. Partial to deep shade. June until frost. Flowers in many colors bloom profusely. Plant bulbs in spring and dig them up to store indoors for the winter. Best in pots and window boxes or moist, shady areas.

Buddleia (in varieties) (butterfly bush). 6 feet. Full sun. August–September. Usually purple flowers attract butterflies. A woody shrub that dies back to the ground each fall in Iowa. Choose varieties carefully for hardiness.

Campanula medium (Canterbury bells). 3 feet. Full sun. June. An old-fashioned favorite biennial in pink, blue, and white.

Campanula persicifolia (willow bellflower). 3 feet. Full sun. July–August. White and blue bell-shaped blooms. Very reliable.

Canna (in varieties). 3–4 feet. Full sun. June until frost. Tall spikes of red to yellow flowers bloom until frost. Use as a background flower. Plant from bulbs in spring, and dig them up to store indoors in fall.

Chrysanthemum coccineum (florist's pyrethrum). 3 feet. Full sun. June–July. White and pink flowers make an excellent cut flower. Very reliable.

Cimicifuga racemosa (black snakeroot or bugbane). 3–8 feet. Full sun to partial shade. July–August. Tall spikes of white flowers. A coarse and large wildflower, it should be used as a background plant.

Coreopsis lanceolata (tickseed). 2 feet. Full sun. June–August. Bright yellow flowers are excellent for cutting. An Iowa native and very easy. Somewhat drought resistant.

Crocus (in varieties). 6 inches. Full sun to partial shade. April. Many colors. Often blooms while snow is still on the ground. Plant bulbs in fall. Naturalizes well and is easy to grow.

Delphinium (in varieties) (delphinium). 6 feet. Full sun. June–July. Tall spikes of blue or white flowers are good for back of the border.

Delphinium grandiflorum chinese (slender Siberian larkspur). 3 feet. Full sun. June. Spikes of blue or white flowers. Reliable and an excellent cut flower.

Dendranthema grandiflorum (chrysanthemum) (in varieties). 2 feet and up. Full sun. August–October. The classic autumn chrysanthemum, it comes in many colors and petal shapes. Very easy, but sometimes dies out during harsh winters. Excellent cut flower.

Dicentra eximia (fringed or everblooming bleeding-heart). 10 inches. Partial shade. June–September. Nodding pink flowers bloom almost continuously starting in June. Good for shady areas.

Dicentra spectablis (common bleeding-heart). 2 feet. Partial shade. May–June. Pink heartlike flowers. Foliage dies to the ground shortly after blooming. Easy.

Digitalis (in varieties) (foxglove). 3 feet. Sun to partial shade. June–July. Bell-shaped flowers on tall spikes make this biennial excellent for the back of shady borders. Many colors. Does best in northeast Iowa.

Echinacea purpurea (purple coneflower). 2 feet. Full sun. July–September. These native plants have deep purple-pink or white petals. Easy and drought resistant.

Eupatorium (in varieties) (Joe-pye weed). 3 feet. Full sun. August–September. Blue or white flowers make good cut flowers. Some cultivars are Iowa natives.

Gaillardia aristata (gaillardia). 2 feet. Full sun. June–October. Flowers in red, yellows, and oranges. Excellent cut flower and very easy.

Gladiolius (in varieties). 2–6 feet. Full sun. July–October. Excellent cut flowers in every color. Plant in spring, and dig up bulbs in fall.

Gypsophila paniculata (baby's breath). 3 feet. Full sun. July. White or pink flowers are excellent filler for arrangements. Dries well and is drought resistant.

Helenium autumnale (sneezeweed). 5 feet. Full sun. August–September. Good background flower in red, yellow, and orange. Excellent cut flower. Drought resistant.

Helianthus decapetalus (double thinleaf sunflower). 4 feet. Full sun. August–September. Large yellow flowers. Good cut flower. Drought resistant.

Hemerocallis (in varieties) (daylily). 4 feet. Full sun to partial shade. June–July. Many colors, mainly yellows, reds, and oranges. Each flower lasts one day. Very easy.

Heuchera sanguinea (in varieties) (coralbells). 2 feet. Full sun to partial shade. May–June. Small white, pink, or red flowers are excellent for cutting. Dries well. Good edging flower and very easy.

Hosta (in varieties). 2 feet. Partial shade to deep shade. July–August. Grown for its foliage but sends up purple or white flowers. Very easy.

Hyacinthus (in varieties) (hyacinth). 1 foot. Full sun. April–May. Very fragrant flowers in blue, pink, and white. Plant bulbs in fall. Dies out after a few years.

Iris germanica (German bearded iris). 3 feet. Full sun. May–June. Many colors available. Good cut flower. Prevent blight that occurs late in the season by treating foliage with wettable sulfur in late April or early May. Tolerates dry conditions.

Iris siberica (Siberian iris). 3 feet. Full sun. May–June. Blue, purple, and white flowers. Very easy and disease resistant. Good cut flower. Tolerates dry conditions.

Liatris pycnostachya (Kansas gayfeather). 2 feet. Full sun to partial shade. August–September. Spikes of red to purple flowers are almost fluorescent. Very reliable native plant. Excellent cut flower.

Liatris spicata (blazing star or gayfeather). 2 feet. Full sun. July. Spikes of magenta or white flowers. Excellent cut flowers. Tolerates dry conditions.

Lilium auratum (in varieties) (Goldband lily). 4–8 feet. Partial shade. June–July. Fragrant flowers in various colors. Do best when left undisturbed for many years. Very reliable. Excellent cut flower.

Lilium × macalatum (in varieties) (Thunberg lilies). 1–2 feet. Full sun. June–July. Fragrant flowers in various colors but usually red, orange, or yellow. Very reliable. Excellent cut flower.

Lilium speciosum (in varieties). 2–4 feet. Partial shade. August–September. Fragrant flowers in various colors. Very reliable. Good cut flower.

Lilium tigrinum or *Lilium lancifolium* (tiger lily). 2–5 feet. Full sun to partial shade. July, August, or September. Flowers are usually bright orange to red with black dots. Good cut flower.

Lilium × hybrids (in varieties). 2–4 feet. Full sun to partial shade. June–July. Usually yellow, red, and orange flowers. Very reliable. Good cut flowers.

Linum perenne (perennial flax). 18 inches. Full sun to partial shade. June–July. Clear blue flowers hover over very fine textured blue-green foliage.

Lythrum (purple loosestrife). 3–6 feet. Full sun to partial shade. June–August. Tall, bushy plant with deep pink spikes. Wild forms are classified as a noxious weed in Iowa, so be certain to plant a hybridized, nonseeding variety, such as "Morden's Pink." Good cut flower, drought resistant, and very easy.

Mertensia virginica (Virginia bluebells). 2 feet. Partial shade. March–April. Native Iowa wildflower. Foliage dies back in early summer.

Monarda didyma (bee balm or Oswego tea). 3 feet. Full sun to partial shade. June–August. Flowers are various shades of red. Easy. Good cut flower.

Muscari (in varieties) (grape hyacinth). 6 inches. Full sun. April–May. Bright blue flower clusters that resemble grapes. Plant bulbs in fall. Easy.

Narcissus (in varieties) (daffodil). 1 foot. Full sun. April–May. Fairly fragrant yellow or white flowers. Excellent cut flowers. Naturalize well. Plant bulbs in fall. Easy.

Nepeta mussini (Persian catmint). 1 foot. Full sun. June–October. Small blue flowers and gray-green foliage make this an excellent edging flower. Also good for retaining walls and rock gardens.

Oenothera missouriensis (evening primrose). 10 inches. Partial shade. June–August. Bright yellow flowers close up at night. Good edging, rock garden, or stone wall flower. Drought resistant.

Paeonia albiflora (peony or Chinese peony). 3 feet. Partial shade to full sun. May–June. Reds, pinks, and whites. Some are very fragrant. Very easy.

Papaver orientale (Oriental poppy). 2 feet. Full sun. May–June. Foliage dies to the ground after blooming and looks ratty. Best used interplanted with other perennials that will cover the dying foliage, such as Shasta daisies.

Phlox divaricata (sweet William). 10 inches. Full sun. May–June. Fragrant lavender flowers. Good cut flower.

Phlox paniculata (in varieties) (garden or summer phlox). 3–4 feet. Full sun or partial shade. July–August. Many colors but primarily white, pink, and red. Very hardy but susceptible to powdery mildew. Easy.

Phlox subulata (creeping or moss phlox). 6 inches. Full sun. April–May. Comes in many colors. Good cut flower. Excellent as a ground cover, in retaining walls, or in rock gardens.

Physotegia virginiana (obedience plant or false dragon's-head). 3 feet. Full sun to partial shade. August–September. Pink or white flowers. Spreads rapidly and can be invasive. Drought tolerant. Good cut flower.

Platycodon grandiflorum (balloonflower). 3 feet. Full sun to half shade. June–August. Blue or white flowers. Very reliable.

Rudbeckia (black-eyed Susan). 2–4 feet. Full sun. July–September. Golden daisylike flowers have brown centers. Excellent for cutting. "Goldsturm" is one of the best varieties of this Iowa native. Easy.

Scabiosa caucasica (pincushion flower). 18 inches. Full sun. June–September. White and blue flowers. Good cut flower.

Scilla siberica (Siberian squill). 6 inches. Full sun to partial shade. April. Tiny flowers are deep vivid blue and effective when planted in large masses. Naturalizes well. Very easy.

Sedum (in varieties). 6–18 inches. Full sun to partial shade. May–August. Flowers of different colors. Succulent-looking foliage. Many make good edging plants. Drought tolerant. Popular "Autumn Joy" is very easy and a good cut flower.

Solidago (goldenrod). 2–6 feet. Full sun. July–
  August. Arched golden sprays are excellent for
  cutting. Drought tolerant and doesn't mind
  poor soils. Iowa native. Hybrids bought at
  nurseries aren't invasive, and this plant, despite
  popular notions, doesn't bother allergies.

Tulipa (in varieties) (tulip). 1 foot. Full sun. April–
  May. Popular bulbs in many flower shapes and
  colors. Plant in fall. Bulbs tend to die out in a
  few years, but life can be extended by choosing
  varieties known to last longer and planting in
  rich, crumbly soil with excellent drainage.

Veronica (in varieties) (speedwell). 3 feet. Full sun.
  June–August. Usually blue or white spike
  flowers. Very reliable and hardy. Excellent cut
  flower.

Vinca minor (creeping periwinkle). 3 inches. Partial
  shade to full sun. April. Covered with blue
  flowers. Excellent ground cover. Easy.

Viola cornuta (in varieties) (horned violet). 6 inches.
  Full sun to partial shade. May–October. Many
  different colors and fragrant. Good edging
  flower.

Yucca filamentosa (yucca). 6 feet. Full sun. June–
  July. Distinctive spiky foliage sends up fragrant,
  creamy spikes. Good plant to use for an accent
  or contrast. Easy and drought tolerant.

BEST TREES AND SHRUBS FOR IOWA

SMALL DECIDUOUS TREES

Acer campestre (hedge maple)

Acer griseum (paperbark maple)

Acer miyabei (Miyabe maple)

Acer tataricum (Tatar maple)

Acer triflorum (three-flowered maple)

Acer truncatum (Shantung maple)

Amelanchier spp. (serviceberry)

Amelanchier × *grandiflora* (apple serviceberry)

Carpinus betulus (European hornbeam)

Carpinus caroliniana (American hornbeam)

Cornus alternifolia (pagoda dogwood)

Cornus mas (cornelian cherry dogwood)

Cornus racemosa (gray dogwood)

Crataegus crus-galli inermis (cockspur hawthorn)

Crataegus phaenopyrum (Washington hawthorn)

Hamamelis virginiana (common witch hazel)

Maackia amurensis (Amur maackia)

Magnolia tomentosa (star magnolia)

Magnolia × *loebneri* (Loebner magnolia)

Magnolia × *soulangiana* (saucer magnolia)

Malus spp. (crabapple)

Ostrya virginiana (American hophornbeam)

Pyrus calleryana (Callery pear)

Sorbus alnifolia (Korean mountain ash)

Syringa reticulata (Japanese tree lilac)

LARGE DECIDUOUS TREES

Acer platanoides (Norway maple)

Acer rubrum (red maple)

Acer saccharum (sugar maple)

Acer truncatum × *platanoides* "Pacific Sunset" (hybrid maple)

Acer × *freemanii* "Autumn Blaze" (Freeman maple)

Betula lenta (sweet birch)

Betula nigra (river birch)

Cladrastis kentukea (yellowwood)

Fraxinus americana (white ash)

Fraxinus pennsylvanica (green ash)

Ginkgo biloba (ginkgo)

Gymnocladus dioicus (Kentucky coffee tree)

Magnolia acuminata (cucumbertree magnolia)

Quercus macrocarpa (bur oak)

Quercus rubra (red oak)

Tilia americana (American linden)

Tilia cordata (littleleaf linden)

CONIFEROUS TREES AND SHRUBS

Abies concolor (white fir)

Larix decidua (European larch)

Picea abies (Norway spruce)

Picea glauca (white spruce)

Picea omorika (Serbian spruce)

Picea pungens (Colorado spruce)

Pinus bungeana (lacebark pine)

Pinus cembra (Swiss stone pine)

Pinus koraiensis (Korean pine)

Pinus mugo (Mugo pine)

Pinus strobus (eastern white pine)

Pinus sylvestris (Scotch pine)

Pseudotsuga menziesii (Douglas fir)

Taxodium distichum (baldcypress)

Taxus baccata (English yew)

Taxus cuspidata (Japanese yew)

Taxus × media (Anglo-Japanese yew)

Thuja occidentalis (eastern or American arbor vitae)

Thuja occidentalis "Techny" (Techny arbor vitae)

Tsuga canadensis (eastern hemlock)

DECIDUOUS SHRUBS

Acer ginnala "Bailey Compact" (Amur maple "Bailey Compact")

Aesculus parviflora (bottlebrush buckeye)

Amelanchier alnifolia "Regent" ("Regent" serviceberry)

Aronia arbutifolia "Brilliantissima" (red chokeberry)

Aronia melanocarpa elata (black chokeberry)

Clethra alnifolia (summersweet clethra)

Cornus mas (cornelian cherry dogwood)

Cornus racemosa (gray dogwood)

Cornus sericea "Cardinal" (Red osier dogwood)

Corylus americana (American filbert or hazelnut)

Cotoneaster lucidus (hedge cotoneaster)

Deutzia gracilis (slender deutzia)

Euonymus alatus (winged euonymus)

Forsythia "Meadowlark" or "Sunrise" (forsythia)

Fothergilla gardenii "Mt. Airy" (dwarf fothergilla)

Hamamelis vernalis (vernal witch hazel)

Hamamelis virginiana (common witch hazel)

Hibiscus syriacus (shrub althea)

Hydrangea quercifolia (oakleaf hydrangea)

Ilex glabra Nordic (inkberry)

Ilex verticillata (winterberry)

Lonicera xylosteum "Hedge King" or "Emerald Mound" (honeysuckle)

Philadelphus × "Snowgoose" (mock orange)

Physocarpus opulifolius "Dart's Golden" (ninebark)

Physocarpus opulifolius nanus (dwarf ninebark)

Rhus aromatica (fragrant sumac)

Rhus typhina "Laciniata" (cutleaf staghorn sumac)

Sorbaria sorbifolia (Ural falsespiraea)

Spiraea japonica "Alpina" or "Little Princess" (Japanese spiraea)

Spiraea × *bumalda* "Anthony Waterer" (Bumald spiraea)

Spiraea × "Goldmound" (goldmound spiraea)

Syringa meyeri "Palibin" (Meyer lilac)

Syringa vulgaris (common lilac)

Syringa × *prestoniae* "James McFarlane" or "Donald Wyman" (Preston lilac)

Viburnum dentatum Chicago Lustre or Northern Burgundy (arrowwood or southern viburnum)

Viburnum lantana "Mohican" (wayfaringtree viburnum)

Viburnum prunifolium (blackhaw viburnum)

Viburnum rufidulum (rusty blackhaw viburnum)

Viburnum trilobum "Compactum" or "Wentworth" (American cranberry viburnum)

Viburnum × *juddii* (Judd viburnum)

Viburnum × *rhytidophylloides* "Allegheny" or "Willowwood" (viburnum)

Source: Iowa State University Horticulture Extension.

BEST PERENNIAL VINES FOR IOWA

Aristolchia durior (Dutchman's pipe). 30 feet. Partial shade to full sun. Summer. Vigorous, twining vine that requires strong support. Flowers look like little pipes.

Campsis (trumpetvine). 25 feet. Partial to full sun. Summer. Not always hardy in Zone 4. *Campsis radicans* is a vigorous native vine that needs a very sturdy support. *Campsis* × *tagliabunda* "Mme. Galen" has the same characteristics as *Campsis radicans* but with larger flowers and tamer habit. Climbs by aerial roots that cling to walls, fences, etc.

Celastrus (bittersweet). 15–25 feet. Full sun. Fall. Oriental bittersweet (*Celastrus obiculatus*) is very vigorous. Hardy in Zone 5 in very sheltered sites. Chinese bittersweet (*Celastrus rosthornianus* or *loeseneri*) is hardy through Zone 4. American bittersweet (*Celastrus scandens*) is a native plant, hardy through Zone 3, and is very vigorous. All need a large, sturdy support. Need to plant male and female plants near each other to get the distinctive orange fall fruits.

Clematis (clematis). 6–20 feet. Full sun. Summer–fall. Many species and cultivars available. *Clematis* × *jackmannii* is very popular. Sweet autumn clematis is covered with very small cream-colored flowers and is highly fragrant. When growing clematis, the saying goes, put them "with their feet in the shade and their heads in the sun." Young plants often take three or so years to bloom, and established plants resent transplanting. Hardy Zones 3–5.

Hedera helix (English ivy). 20 feet. Full sun to partial shade. No flower. Hardy in warmer parts of Zone 5 and colder parts if mulched with straw and placed in a protected site. Evergreen. Good cultivars for Iowa include "Baltica," "Bulgaria," and "Ogallala."

Lonicera (honeysuckle). 15–20 feet. Partial shade to full sun. Summer. Several species available, most of which are hardy to Zone 5. Limber honeysuckle (*Lonceria dioica*) is hardy to Zone 2. Twining vines produce flowers in red, purple, yellow, and orange.

Parthenocissus quinquefolia (Virginia creeper or woodbine). 35 feet. Full sun. No flower. A vigorous native that clings with adhesive disks. Produces fruit that looks like clusters of small grapes. Bright red fall color.

Parthenocissus tricuspidata (Boston ivy or Japanese creeper). 25 feet. Full sun to partial shade. No flower. Hardy to Zone 5 but often does well in sheltered sites in Zone 4. Grows densely with adhesive disks that cling to structures. Lustrous leaves and bright red fall color.

Polygonum auberti (silver lace vine). 25 feet. Partial shade to full sun. Late summer. Hardy to Zone 5 and protected sites in Zone 4. Fast-growing twining vine. Fragrant white flowers and showy racemes.

BEST GROUND COVERS FOR IOWA

Aegopodium podogaria (goutweed or bishop's-weed). 2 inches. Partial shade to full sun. Dies to the ground each winter but produces small white flowers in June. Spreads easily and can become invasive.

Ajuga reptans (carpet bugle). 4 inches. Partial shade. May–June. Hardy to Zone 5. Forms a shiny carpet with deep blue, spiked flowers. Cultivars with variegated leaves now available.

Asarum (wild ginger). 8 inches. Partial shade. Spring. Good for relatively moist areas under trees. Grown for its heart-shaped leaves, but tiny reddish flowers appear at base of plant.

Coronilla varia (crownvetch). 2 feet. Full sun. Early summer. Seen primarily along Iowa's roadsides, spreads vigorously, and is best used in large areas where it can sprawl.

Lamium (dead nettle). 6 inches. Partial shade to full sun. Summer. Heart-shaped leaves with many variegations. Produce small pink or white flowers. "Beacon Silver" has striking gray-silver markings.

Vinca minor (creeping periwinkle). 6 inches. Partial shade to full sun. May. Produces small blue flowers above evergreen, glossy foliage.

MAIL-ORDER SUPPLY COMPANIES

B & D Lilies
330 P St.
Port Townsend, WA 98368
206-385-1738
Specializes in lilies; more than 200 varieties are available.

Bluestone Perennials
7211 Middle Ridge Rd.
Madison, OH 44057
1-800-852-5243
Wide variety of perennials and other established plants.

Burpee Seed
300 Park Ave.
Warminster, PA 18974
215-674-4900
General seeds, established plants, and supplies.

The Cook's Garden
P.O. Box 535
Londonderry, VT 05148
802-824-3400
Wide variety of unusual vegetables and other edible plants.

Gardener's Eden
P.O. Box 7307
San Francisco, CA 94120-7307
1-800-822-9600
Established plants and bulbs, but primarily upscale and unusual garden supplies, accessories, gifts, and furniture.

Gardener's Supply Company
128 Intervale Rd.
Burlington, VT 05401
802-863-1700
Variety of practical and innovative gardening supplies and accessories.

The Garden Grow Co.
P.O. Box 278, 6500 Hanna Rd.
Independence, OR 97351
503-838-2811
Organic gardening supplies.

Gardens Alive!
5100 Schenley Pl.
Lawrenceburg, IN 47025
812-537-8650
Organic gardening supplies.

Gurney Seed and Nursery
110 Capital St.
Yankton, SD 57079
605-665-1671
General seeds, established plants, and supplies.

Heard Gardens
5355 Merle Hay Rd.
Johnston, IA 50131
515-276-4533
Specializes in lilacs—nearly 40 varieties—but has
many other plants available. A visit to their grounds
in May and June is worth the trip.

Henry Field Seed and Nursery
415 N. Burnett
Shenandoah, IA 51602
605-665-4491
General seeds, established plants, and supplies.

Jackson and Perkins
P.O. Box 1028
Medford, OR 97501
1-800-292-4769
Upscale supplier of established plants, gardening
gifts, accessories, and garden furniture. Wide
selection of roses makes it a must for rose fanciers.

Jung Quality Seeds
No street address needed
Randolph, WI 53957
414-326-4100
Seeds, established plants, bulbs, and supplies.

Park's Seed Company
P.O. Box 31
Greenwood, SC 29648-0046
1-800-845-3369
Primarily flower and vegetable seeds but some
established plants and bulbs as well.

The Roseraie at Bayfields
P.O. Box R
Waldoboro, ME 04572
207-832-6330
Specializes in "practical roses for hard places."

Schreiner's Iris Gardens
3654 Quinaby Rd. N.E.
Salem, OR 97303
1-800-525-2367
More than 300 iris varieties available.

Shady Oaks Nursery
112 10th Ave. S.E.
Waseca, MN 56093
507-835-5033
A wide selection of shrubs, perennials, ground covers, and other plants suited to shady areas. A must for anyone with a shady yard.

Shepherd's Garden Seeds
30 Irene St.
Torrington, CT 06790
203-482-3638
Specializes in unusual varieties of fruits, herbs, and vegetables. Extensive and unusual lettuce selection.

Smith and Hawken
25 Corte Madera
Mill Valley, CA 94941
415-383-2000
Some established plants and bulbs with lots of upscale garden supplies, gifts, clothing, furniture, and accessories.

Stark Bros.
P.O. Box 10
Louisiana, MO 63353
1-800-325-4180
Primarily fruit and nut trees and other fruit-bearing plants.

Tomato Growers Supply
P.O. Box 2237
Fort Myers, FL 33902
813-768-1119
Specializing in tomatoes with more than 200 different varieties and 50 varieties of peppers. Some gardening supplies and books.

Van Bourgondien
P.O. Box 1000, 245 Farmingdale Rd.
Babylon, NY 11702-0598
1-800-622-9997
General established plants with extensive bulb
selections.

Vermont Wildflower Farm
R.R. 7
Charlotte, VT 05445
802-425-3500
Catalogs and information for planting wildflowers,
especially meadows of wildflowers.

Wayside Gardens
1 Garden Lane
Hodges, SC 29695-0001
1-800-845-1124
Hardy flowering plants, shrubs, trees, and other
plants. Wide selection of roses.

White Flower Farm
P.O. Box 50, Route 63
Litchfield, CT 06759-0050
1-800-944-9624
Upscale established plants and gardening gifts and
supplies.

Worm's Way Garden Supply
3151 S. Highway 446
Bloomington, IN 47401
1-800-274-9676
Indoor and hydroponic gardening supplies.

IOWA GARDENS TO VISIT

Bellevue Butterfly Garden

A half mile south of Bellevue, off U.S. 52 in Bellevue State Park.

Designed specifically to attract butterflies by providing nectar plants for adult butterflies and host plants for caterpillars. Fifty species of butterflies visit the one-acre garden each summer. The park also contains a three-acre prairie preserve, a nature center, and a scenic view of the Mississippi River atop a 300-foot bluff.

Park hours are 5 A.M. to 10:30 P.M. seven days a week. No fee. 319-872-4019.

Bickelhaupt Arboretum, Clinton

340 S. 14th St.

A private arboretum on 14 acres of rolling hills through which winds a creek. More than 2,000 specimens of native or hardy plants, including collections of flowering crabapples, lilacs, and shrub roses and dwarf and rare conifers. Includes an outdoor amphitheater, education center, plant conservatory, and lending library.

Vehicles available for people with disabilities. Education center is open from 9 A.M. to 6 P.M., and the gardens are open from dawn to dusk daily. No fee. 319-242-4771.

Brucemore Historical Site, Cedar Rapids

2160 Linden Drive S.E.

A National Trust for Historic Preservation property that includes a Queen Anne–style estate and 26 acres of lawns, historic formal gardens, and a duck pond. Includes a 1920s English-style country garden with plant varieties and old roses used in that era.

Mansion hours are Tuesday through Saturday, 10 A.M. to 3 P.M. Tours are on the hour. Admission is $5 for adults and $2 for students ages 6 through 18. Grounds can be visited at no charge. 319-362-7375.

Des Moines Botanical Center

909 E. River Drive, Des Moines. Take Pennsylvania Ave. exit off Interstate 235, then follow signs.

Under a 150-foot dome are 1,500 species of tropical and subtropical plants, bonsai, and seasonal displays of flowers. Outdoors, enjoy a pretty view of the river, an herb garden, a cactus and succulent garden, and a courtyard Oriental garden.

The outdoor gardens are free and open any time. The indoor center is open 10 A.M. to 6 P.M. Monday through Thursday; 10 A.M. to 9 P.M. Friday; 10 A.M. to 5 P.M. Saturday and Sunday. Admission is $1.50 for adults, 75¢ for those over 65, 50¢ for ages 6 to 18 and students with ID, and free for children under 6. 515-242-2934.

Dubuque Arboretum and Botanical Gardens
3800 Arboretum Drive in Marshall Park
Nearly 52 acres are divided into separate gardens for roses, ornamental trees and shrubs, perennials and annuals, and prairie wildflowers and grasses; a shade garden and woodland trail; three waterfalls; fruit and nut orchards; a dwarf conifer collection; and a home gardening learning center. Its rose collection has earned several awards, and with 750 varieties of hostas, it contains the largest public hosta collection in the U.S. A Japanese garden is planned.

Open May to November, 8 A.M. to dusk. Vehicles available for people with disabilities. Guided tours $1 per person, otherwise no fee. 319-556-2100.

Greenwood Park Rose Garden, Des Moines
48th St. and Grand Ave.
Showcases nearly 4,000 roses, nearly every species that will grow in Iowa.
Open dawn to dusk. No fee.

Heritage Farm, Decorah
5 1/2 miles north of Decorah on Highway 52, then 1 mile east on N. Winn Rd.
An organic preservation garden containing more than 2,000 varieties of heirloom vegetables, fruits, and flowers. Also the headquarters of Seed Savers Exchange, a nonprofit organization devoted to preserving historic vegetable and fruit varieties from around the world.

Visitors are welcome from June 1 through September 30. On weekdays from 9 A.M. to 5 P.M. a gardener is available to answer questions. Special tours arranged for $1 per person. 319-382-5990.

Iowa Arboretum, rural Boone County
1875 Peach Ave., 2 1/2 miles west and 2 miles south of Luther. Take U.S. Highway 169 or Iowa Highway 17 to Boone County Road E-57 and follow signs.

Containing a "library of living plants," the 300-acre arboretum's mission is to demonstrate the plants best adapted to the soils and climate of Iowa. Hundreds of species of trees, shrubs, and flowering plants. Plants are grouped by type: small shade trees, ornamental deciduous shrubs, herbs, perennials, hostas, etc. Also contains a learning center, gazebo, and butterfly and water gardens.

Open dawn to dusk. Admission is $2. 515-795-3216.

Reiman Gardens, Ames

1407 Elwood Dr., just south of the ISU Cyclone Stadium

Five acres developed on a 14-acre site. Extensive Griffith Buck rose collection (extremely hardy roses bred by an ISU professor), 300 commercially available rose varieties, including the All-America Rose Selection winners, an herb garden, a wetlands garden, a perennials collection, and several thousand annuals.

Gardens open dawn to dusk April through October. Office open 8 A.M. to 5 P.M. Monday through Friday. No fee. 515-294-2710.

Riverside Gardens, Monticello

Northeast edge of Monticello on U.S. Highway 151

This 5-acre garden and 2 1/2-acre wetland is maintained by volunteers. Includes annuals, perennials, cacti, ornamental grasses, a gazebo, an arbor, a wishing well, benches, and brick walks donated by Monticello residents.

Open dawn to dusk. No fee.

Stampe Lilac Gardens, Davenport

Locust St. and Fernwood Ave. in Duck Creek Park

One of the largest lilac plantings (5 acres) in the country. Peaks in mid-May.

Open dawn to dusk. No fee.

Terrace Hill Gardens, Des Moines

2300 Grand Ave.

Lattice fences and arbors accent the Victorian-style garden beds that include 2,000 perennials, old roses, and old-fashioned annuals. Tours are Tuesday through Saturday, 10 A.M. to 1:30 P.M. Admission is $3 for those 13 and older, $1 for ages 6 to 12, and free for children under 6. 515-281-3604.

Vander Veer Park and Conservatory, Davenport
215 W. Central Park Ave.

Nearly 2,000 roses as well as a tropical plant conservatory, flower beds, a fountain, and a lagoon on 33 acres.

The conservatory is open from 10 A.M. to 4 P.M.; gardens open during daylight hours. No fee.

Waterworks Park, Des Moines
Fleur and Locust Sts.

One of the country's finest collections of flowering crabapple trees and an extensive collection of lilacs. Peaks in early May. Open dawn to dusk. No fee. 515-283-8791.

ISU HORTICULTURE ANSWER LINE

A hotline based at Iowa State University and staffed by horticulture professionals. You can ask your gardening and landscaping questions from 10 A.M. to noon and 1 to 4:30 P.M. Monday through Friday, with extended summer hours. The Hortline number is 515-294-3108. Or e-mail the Hortline specialists at hortline@iastate.edu.

IOWA GARDEN CLUB MEMBERSHIP INFORMATION

For information on joining your local garden club or plant society, contact the Iowa State Horticultural Society, Wallace State Office Building, 502 E. 9th Street, Des Moines, IA 50319-0058, 515-281-5402.

COUNTY EXTENSION OFFICES

Your local county extension office is an excellent source of free or low-cost gardening brochures and other plant information. County extension offices also coordinate Master Gardener Classes, a low-cost series of classes on gardening. Here's how to contact the extension office in your county, including e-mail addresses as of July 1996.

Adair
705 NE 6th St.
Greenfield, IA 50849
515-743-8412
x1dhall@exnet.iastate.edu

Adams
603 7th St.
Corning, IA 50841
515-322-3184
x1cnelso@exnet.iastate.edu

Allamakee
21 Allamakee St.
Waukon, IA 52172
319-568-6345
x1gruenh@exnet.iastate.edu

Appanoose
North 12th & Washington
Centerville, IA 52544
515-856-3885
x1swack@exnet.iastate.edu

Audubon
608 Market St.
Audubon, IA 50025
712-563-4239
x1leblen@exnet.iastate.edu

Benton
808 W. 9th St.
Vinton, IA 52349
319-472-4739
x1fisch@exnet.iastate.edu
or x1dwiley@exnet.iastate.edu

Black Hawk
3420 University #B
Waterloo, IA 50701
319-234-6811
x1loenser@exnet.iastate.edu

Boone
603 Story St.
Boone, IA 50036
515-432-3882
x1wrage@exnet.iastate.edu

Bremer
P.O. Box 49
Tripoli, IA 50676
319-882-4275
x1jdill@exnet.iastate.edu

Buchanan
1413 1st St. W, Suite B
Independence, IA 50644
319-334-7161
x1niiche@exnet.iastate.edu

Buena Vista
P.O. Box 820
Storm Lake, IA 50588
712-732-5056
x1rhonda@exnet.iastate.edu

Butler
P.O. Box 368
Allison, IA 50602
319-267-2707
x1derdzi@exnet.iastate.edu

Calhoun
521 4th St., P.O. Box 233
Rockwell City, IA 50579
712-297-8611
x1clancy@exnet.iastate.edu

Carroll
1240 D Heires Ave.
Carroll, IA 51401
712-792-2364
x1molito@exnet.iastate.edu

Cass
1205 Sunnyside Lane
Atlantic, IA 50022
712-243-1132
x1hall@exnet.iastate.edu

Cedar
120 E. 5th
Tipton, IA 52772
319-886-6157
x1long@exnet.iastate.edu

Cerro Gordo
2023 S. Federal
Mason City, IA 50401
515-423-0844
x1kuhl@exnet.iastate.edu

Cherokee
921 S. 2nd St.
Cherokee, IA 51012
712-225-6196
x1avis@exnet.iastate.edu

Chickasaw
104 E. Main
New Hampton, IA 50659
515-394-2174
x1prouty@exnet.iastate.edu

Clarke
117 1/2 S. Main
Osceola, IA 50213
515-342-3316
x1mbeck@exnet.iastate.edu

Clay
110 W. 4th St.
Spencer, IA 51301
712-262-2264
x1lohman@exnet.iastate.edu

Clayton
133 S. Main
Elkader, IA 52043
319-245-1451
x1hosch@exnet.iastate.edu

Clinton
331 E. 8th
Dewitt, IA 52742
319-659-5125
x1hank@exnet.iastate.edu

Crawford
35 S. Main
Denison, IA 51442
712-263-4697
x1weeda@exnet.iastate.edu

Dallas
905 Main
Adel, IA 50003
515-993-4281
x1lnelso@exnet.iastate.edu

Davis
106 N. Dodge
Bloomfield, IA 52537
515-664-2730
x1mussel@exnet.iastate.edu

Decatur
309 N. Main
Leon, IA 50144
515-446-4723
x1vanlr@exnet.iastate.edu

Delaware
115 E. Delaware
Manchester, IA 52057
319-927-4201
x1hanso@exnet.iastate.edu

Des Moines
900 Osborn
Burlington, IA 52601
319-754-7556
x1buzz@exnet.iastate.edu

Dickinson
1610A 18th St.
Spirit Lake, IA 51360
712-336-3488
x1janach@exnet.iastate.edu

ISU PLANT
DISEASE CLINIC

Operated by Iowa State University Extension plant pathologists, this sometimes-free service allows you to mail in samples of diseased plants for diagnosis. In some cases, a $5 to $10 fee is charged for more detailed analysis. See page 68 for more information on how to send in a sample. Write or phone: Plant Disease Clinic, 323 Bessey Hall, Iowa State University, Ames, IA 50011, 515-294-0581; e-mail: sickplant@iastate.edu. Insect pest questions can be answered via e-mail: insects@iastate.edu.

Dubuque
2600 Dodge St.
Dubuque, IA 52001
319-583-6496
x1berna@exnet.iastate.edu

Emmett
26 S. 17th St.
Estherville, IA 51334
712-362-3434
x1holle@exnet.iastate.edu

Fayette
P.O. Box 700
Fayette, IA 52142
319-425-3331
x1burk@exnet.iastate.edu

Floyd
615 Beck St.
Charles City, IA 50616
515-228-1453
x1philip@exnet.iastate.edu

Franklin
3 1st Ave. N.W.
Hampton, IA 50441
515-456-4811
x1bjpete@exnet.iastate.edu

Fremont
P.O. Box 420
Sidney, IA 51652
712-374-2351
x1mcclur@exnet.iastate.edu

Greene
1401 N. Elm
Jefferson, IA 50129
515-386-2138
x1hertel@exnet.iastate.edu

Grundy
703 F Ave. Suite #1
Grundy Center, IA 50638
319-824-6979
x1allanv@exnet.iastate.edu

Guthrie
411 State St.
Guthrie Center, IA 50115
515-747-2276
x1pchar@exnet
or x1smitcr@exnet.iastate.edu

Hamilton
735 2nd
Webster City, IA 50595
515-832-9597
x1bshaw@exnet.iastate.edu

Hancock
327 W. 8th St.
Garner, IA 50438
515-923-2856
x1jhhill@exnet.iastate.edu

Hardin
P.O. Box 349
Eldora, IA 50627
515-858-5425
x1msmith@exnet.iastate.edu

Harrison
304 E. 7th
Logan, IA 51546
712-644-2105
x1guge@exnet.iastate.edu

Henry
101 S. Jefferson
Mount Pleasant, IA 52641
319-385-8126
x1jsmith@exnet.iastate.edu

Howard
132 1st St. Ave. W.
Cresco, IA 52136
319-547-3001
x1arendt@exnet.iastate.edu

Humboldt
727 Sumner, P.O. Box 158
Humboldt, IA 50548
515-332-2201
x1mhoyer@exnet.iastate.edu

Ida
211 Main St.
Ida Grove, IA 51445
712-364-3003
x1warnke@exnet.iastate.edu

Iowa
P.O. Box 146
Marengo, IA 52301
319-642-5504
x1steve@exnet.iastate.edu

Jackson
201 W. Platt
Maquoketa, IA 52060
319-652-4923
x1hains@exnet.iastate.edu

Jasper
550 N. 2nd Ave. W.
Newton, IA 50208
515-792-6433
x1chip@exnet.iastate.edu

Jefferson
P.O. Box 445
Fairfield, IA 52556
515-472-4166
x1bower@exnet.iastate.edu

Johnson
4265 Oak Crest Hill Rd. S.E.
Iowa City, IA 52246
319-337-2145
x1mohlin@exnet.iastate.edu

Jones
605 E. Main, P.O. Box 168
Anamosa, IA 52205
319-462-2791
x1yedlik@exnet.iastate.edu

Kossuth
1121 B Highway 18 E.
Algona, IA 50511
515-295-2469
x1yeske@exnet.iastate.edu

Lee
P.O. Box 70
Donnellson, IA 52625
319-835-5116
x1dodds@exnet.iastate.edu

Linn
655 12th St.
Marion, IA 52302
319-377-9839
x1bigley@exnet.iastate.edu

Louisa
319 Van Buren
Wapello, IA 52653
319-523-2371
x1werner@exnet.iastate.edu

Lucas
R.R. 5, P.O. Box 91
Chariton, IA 50049
515-774-2016
x1beth@exnet.iastate.edu

Lyon
301 1/2 1st St. #202
Rock Rapids, IA 51246
712-472-2576
x1rbens@exnet.iastate.edu

Madison
117 N. 1st St.
Winterset, IA 50273
515-462-1001
x1lake@exnet.iastate.edu

Mahaska
113 A Ave. W.
Oskaloosa, IA 52577
515-673-5841
x1torber@exnet.iastate.edu

Marion
303 1/2 E. Marion
Knoxville, IA 50138
515-842-2014
x1dmill@exnet.iastate.edu

Marshall
3205 S. 6th St.
Marshalltown, IA 50158
515-752-1551
x1helgen@exnet.iastate.edu

Mills
P.O. Box 430
Malvern, IA 51551
712-624-8616
x1obrech@exnet.iastate.edu

Mitchell
509 1/2 State St.
Osage, IA 50461
515-732-5574
x1wubben@exnet.iastate.edu

Monona
119 Iowa Ave.
Onawa, IA 51040
712-423-2175
x1hardi@exnet.iastate.edu

Monroe
107 Benton Ave. E.
Albia, IA 52531
515-932-5612
x1delane@exnet.iastate.edu

Montgomery
400 Bridge, Suite #1
Red Oak, IA 51566
712-623-2592
x1brooke@exnet.iastate.edu

Muscatine
2517 Park Ave.
Muscatine, IA 52761
319-263-5701
x1owen@exnet.iastate.edu

O'Brien
P.O. Box 99
Primghar, IA 51245
712-757-5045
x1rouwen@exnet.iastate.edu

Osceola
839 3rd Ave.
Sibley, IA 51249
712-754-3648
x1welcha@exnet.iastate.edu

Page
311 E. Washington
Clarinda, IA 51632
712-542-5171
x1sanson@exnet.iastate.edu

Palo Alto
1108 Main, P.O. Box 323
Emmetsburg, IA 50536
712-852-2865
x1hammon@exnet.iastate.edu

Plymouth
24 1st St. N.W.
LeMars, IA 51031
712-546-7835
x1frus@exnet.iastate.edu

Pocahontas
P.O. Box 209
Pocahontas, IA 50574
712-335-3103
x1njens@exnet.iastate.edu

Polk
5035 N.E. 14th
Des Moines, IA 50313
515-263-2660
x1hug@exnet.iastate.edu

Pottawattamie, East
120 N. Main
Oakland, IA 51560
712-482-6449
x1dbaker@exnet.iastate.edu
or x1robbie@exnet.iastate.edu

Pottawattamie, West
1600 S. Highway 275
Council Bluffs, IA 51503
712-366-7070
x1oelker@exnet.iastate.edu

Poweshiek
P.O. Box 70
Montezuma, IA 50171
515-623-5188
x1johann@exnet.iastate.edu
or x1arkel@exnet.iastate.edu

Ringold
101 N. Polk
Mount Ayr, IA 50854
515-464-3333
x1judyh@exnet.iastate.edu

Sac
110 S. 6th, Suite D
Sac City, IA 50583
712-662-7131
x1jensen@exnet.iastate.edu

Scott
875 Tanglefoot Lane
Bettendorf, IA 52722
319-359-7577
x1bray@exnet.iastate.edu

Shelby
1105 8th St.
Harlan, IA 51537
712-755-3104
x1fike@exnet.iastate.edu

Sioux
805 Highway 10 W.
Orange City, IA 51041
712-737-4230
x1hero@exnet.iastate.edu

Story
220 H. Ave., P.O. Box 118
Nevada, IA 50201
515-382-6551
x1mannin@exnet.iastate.edu

Tama
P.O. Box 308
Toledo, IA 52342
515-484-2703
x1wlest@exnet.iastate.edu

Taylor
312 Main St.
Bedford, IA 50833
712-523-2137
x1brant@exnet.iastate.edu

Union
105 W. Adams, Suite B
Creston, IA 50801
515-782-8426
x1wasten@exnet.iastate.edu

Van Buren
P.O. Box 456
Keosauqua, IA 52565
319-293-3039
x1mclain@exnet.iastate.edu

Wapello
700 Farm Credit Dr.
Ottumwa, IA 52501
515-682-5491
x1larche@exnet.iastate.edu

Warren
1202 E. 2nd
Indianola, IA 50125
515-961-6237
x1jmr@exnet.iastate.edu

Washington
P.O. Box 29
Washington, IA 52353
319-653-4811
x1nschmi@exnet.iastate.edu

Wayne
P.O. Box 281
Corydon, IA 50060
515-872-1755
x1swartz@exnet.iastate.edu

Webster
29 N. 16th St.
Fort Dodge, IA 50501
515-576-2119
x1patton@exnet.iastate.edu

Winnebago
P.O. Box 47
Thompson, IA 50478
515-584-2261
x1cjp@exnet.iastate.edu

Winneshiek
911 S. Mill
Decorah, IA 52101
319-382-2949
x1horne@exnet.iastate.edu

Woodbury
4301 Sergeant #213
Sioux City, IA 51106
712-276-2157
x1cox@exnet.iastate.edu

Worth
808 Central Ave.
Northwood, IA 50459
515-324-1531
x1djohn@exnet.iastate.edu

Wright
210 1st St. S.W.
Clarion, IA 50525
515-532-3453
x1untied@exnet.iastate.edu

INDEX

euphorbia, 91
European hornbeam, 130
evening primrose, 128
evergreens, 2, 85, 96, 115, 119, 120; pruning, 85, 119
exotic plants, 69
extension offices, county, 144–148

fall color, 106–108; bulbs, 108; perennials, 107–108; shrubs, 107
fall crops, 94
fall gardens, 106
false dragonshead, 128
false spiraea, Ural, 132
February: checklist, 14–15
fencing, 79–80, 81
fern, 61, 63
fertilizer, 22, 34, 42, 88, 93, 96, 113, 118
filbert, American, 131
filler, 90–91
fir: Douglas, 131; white, 131
firethorn shrub, 115
flax, perennial, 127
floating row cover, 14, 17–18
floral fixative, 114
floral foam. *See* Oasis
florist's pyrethrum, 125
flowerpots, 105, 113
flowers: to dry, 114–115; mail-order, 136–139
forcing: bulbs, 3, 15, 100–101; shrubs, 15
forsythia, 15, 91, 131
foxglove, 40, 48, 62, 72, 86

French tarragon, 44
frog, 90
frost, 34, 96, 104; protecting vegetables, 104; removing dead plants, 105
fruit trees, 70; mail-order, 138; rodent protection, 111; suckers and sprouts, 74
fungicide, 53, 74
fungus, 76

garden: accents and structures, 120; clubs, 40, 144; design, 4–6; gifts, 121, 138; journal, 11; records, 11; refuse, 42; supplies, mail-order, 136–139; tools, 14, 21–22, 26, 93; to visit, 140–143; winter, 119–120
garden phlox, 91, 128
gayfeather, 127; Kansas, 126
geranium, 102
German statice, 114
ginkgo, 130
gladiolus, 3, 46, 86, 96, 104
globe amaranth, 114
goat's-beard, 61
godetia, 24, 35
goldenrod, 91, 129
gopher, 82
goutweed, 135
grape hyacinth, 86, 127
grapevine, 24
grass: clippings, 110, 112–113; ornamental, 106, 115, 120; sowing seed, 48; types of, 57
greens, 16, 17, 35; collard, 98; mustard, 74, 94, 98

ground cherry, 107
ground ivy, 37, 78–79, 88, 89
grow light, 20
gypsum, 27, 86

hand saw, 22
hand trowel, 22
hardening off, 20, 46
hardiness: plant, 7–8; USDA zones, 9
hardy geranium, 41, 62
hawthorn: cockspur, 130; Washington, 130
hay, 104
heaving, 8
heliopsis, 41
heliotrope, 102
help, sources of, 144–148
hemlock, eastern, 131
herb, 3, 14, 16, 17, 35, 43–44
herbicide, 29, 37, 67, 79. *See also* weed killer
hoe, 93
holly, 37, 115, 119, 120
hollyhock, 40, 48, 72, 124
honeysuckle, 131, 133; limber, 133
hornbeam: American, 130; European, 130
hose, 21, 77
hosta, 62, 79, 126
hotbed, 98
hotcap, 14
houseplants, 2, 90, 118
hyacinth, 15, 86, 88, 126; forcing, 100
hydrangea, 63, 91; oakleaf, 131

Birds of an Iowa Dooryard
By Althea R. Sherman

A Country So Full of Game:
The Story of Wildlife in Iowa
By James J. Dinsmore

Fragile Giants: A Natural
History of the Loess Hills
By Cornelia F. Mutel

Gardening in Iowa
and Surrounding Areas
By Veronica Lorson Fowler

Iowa Birdlife
By Gladys Black

The Iowa Breeding Bird Atlas
By Laura Spess Jackson,
Carol A. Thompson, and
James J. Dinsmore

Landforms of Iowa
By Jean C. Prior

Land of the Fragile Giants:
Landscapes, Environments, and
Peoples of the Loess Hills
Edited by Cornelia F. Mutel
and Mary Swander

Okoboji Wetlands: A Lesson
in Natural History
By Michael J. Lannoo

Parsnips in the Snow: Talks with
Midwestern Gardeners
By Jane Anne Staw and
Mary Swander

Prairies, Forests, and Wetlands:
The Restoration of Natural
Landscape Communities in Iowa
By Janette R. Thompson

Restoring the Tallgrass Prairie:
An Illustrated Manual for Iowa
and the Upper Midwest
By Shirley Shirley

The Vascular Plants of Iowa:
An Annotated Checklist and
Natural History
By Lawrence J. Eilers
and Dean M. Roosa